HUNTING FOR TRUE WEALTH

Stories and Wisdom from a
Big Game Hunter, Entrepreneur,
Mayor, and Family Man

DAVE YOUNG

Peacock Proud
PRESS
PHOENIX, ARIZONA

Advance Praise for *Hunting for True Wealth*

"This book will help those who study and practice its five principles achieve a 'Rich Life.' Dave Young's concrete examples and principles are so well told. I wish he had written this book years ago—and that I had studied it. I would have bagged a lot more trophies sooner in life!"
–Don Peay, Founder, Sportsmen for Fish and Wildlife

"Hunting for True Wealth is a perfect balance of financial advice mixed with important life lessons. Through Dave Young's incredible hunting stories, you get to experience the real value of hunting for true wealth. I highly recommend this book and hope you'll enjoy Dave's journey as much as I did."
–Nate Randle, CEO at Gabb, Safe phones and watches for kids and teens

"In *Hunting for True Wealth*, Dave Young skillfully tracks the wild terrain of personal finance, drawing striking parallels between big game hunting and wealth management."
–Susan Richards, business owner and philanthropist

"I love Dave Young's tales of both his hunting exploits and his business and investing lessons learned, both for financial success and, especially, for personal happiness. Dave is authentic and obviously dedicated to his children's lives as kids, and now, as successful adults. Anyone interested in financial and personal wealth and happiness should read Dave's book and follow its principles."
–Stan Ricks, Co-founder, Managing Director, Sundance Bay

"Mayor Dave Young has definitely had mind-blowing experiences to back up the critical core values and principles he espouses in *Hunting for True Wealth*. The wisdom he shares from his death-defying adventures will inspire readers to adopt those values as well. Who knew that learning about big game hunting would make talking about investing and finances actually fun?"
–Brenn Bybee, Orem City Manager

"*Hunting for True Wealth* is a treasure—a book worth its weight in gold. Not only do you gain big-time advice and insights about how to build wealth, but you'll become entranced by hair-raising adventures in the jungle and see what causes the most incredible wealth of all—happiness and joy in life. It's a fun read with valuable pearls of wisdom for anyone who wants to master the principles of wealth and life."

–Steven R. Shallenberger, Founder, Becoming Your Best Global Leadership; author *Becoming Your Best: The 12 Principles of Highly Successful Leaders and Do What Matters Most*

"As a fellow hunter who enjoys the beauty of the outdoors, challenge of the hunt, and respect for God's handiwork, I thoroughly enjoyed *Hunting for True Wealth*. It draws the reader in with accounts of thrilling adventure, then artfully shares how intentionally living Dave Young's critical core values brings true wealth, no matter the storm that surrounds you. His connections between adventure, core values, and wealth are pearls of wisdom everyone should seek and live."

–LaNae Millett, Orem City Councilwoman

"I love the perspective Dave Young offers in *Hunting for True Wealth* because happiness isn't obtained in any single accomplishment, but by living life to its fullest with those you love. Dave's insights are worth the read."

–Richard King, Independent Consultant and former President, FATPOT Technologies

*For my wife, Cathy,
and our five children:
Shannon, Katie, Shawn,
Kelli, and Austin*

TABLE OF CONTENTS

MY FIRST ROOKIE MISTAKE, KILLING A DOE

T he first time I shot a deer was a major screw-up.

Back in the day, New Mexico hadn't yet established any education rules or requirements for getting a hunting license. If you could carry a gun, you could go hunting. So, in 1968, when I was just twelve years old, I talked an older group of boys—about seventeen to twenty-three years old—into letting me go deer hunting with them.

Since I was too young to own a gun myself, I borrowed my dad's .30-06, an old, heavy rifle he'd gotten from an army surplus store. He also gave me some bullets, and off I went up a mountain to hunt in the high mountain desert. I'm still kind of shocked my parents let me go hunting with these older guys from church, but somehow, I talked my mom and dad into it. There were five of us, and at age twelve, I felt like I was already grown up.

We camped out and had a great time. Tagging along with these teenagers and young men, one of whom had been in the army, I was pretty excited about the chance to get my first deer.

Before sunrise, we woke up, and everybody took off in different directions. There I was, a young kid all by myself with a gun, hiking the side of a mountain, wearing one of my dad's yellow pullovers. Back then, you had to wear yellow or orange. Now hunters only wear blaze orange.

Quite a ways from the camp, I found this little ravine surrounded by red rock, leafless quakies, pines, and a random cactus here and there. I could hear an occasional squirrel chatter or bird chirp. Otherwise, it was just another quiet fall day.

I'd never shot the .30-06 before, so I decided to start practicing. It had open sights on it, meaning it didn't have a scope, and at the time, the gun was only a little shorter than I was tall. World War II surplus guns weren't designed for efficiency. Looking back, I realize now that gun was a piece of junk, especially in comparison to what I shoot with today.

I wanted to be ready in case a deer showed up. I went through all the motions, although I didn't actually shoot; that would've scared everything away. Pretending a rock or a bush was a deer, I'd bring up the rifle, sight on it, and squeeze the trigger—without a bullet in the chamber.

Spending most of the morning like this, I was a little kid, alone, trying to figure out rifle handling and shooting.

Around midday, I heard a noise above and behind me.

Oh my gosh, I thought, exhilarated. *This is it, a deer.*

I put a bullet in the chamber and got it ready. A deer came into sight, traveling down the ravine...but it was a doe, a female deer. We were hunting for bucks. Doe hunting is illegal.

Getting the doe in my sights, I followed it. Even though I couldn't shoot, it would still be good practice. A moving target. Before it disappeared, I hoped to get a feel for aiming at the right spot behind the animal's shoulder.

On it, on it, on it while it came down the ravine, I squeezed the trigger softly.

Boom!

The gun went off, recoiling hard because I wasn't expecting it, because I wasn't intending to actually discharge the weapon. My heart stopped in surprise.

Holy crap! What just happened?

I'd screwed up.

In my mind, I'd just been going through the same practice motions that I'd been rehearsing all morning. But this was a live gun. I hadn't registered that I'd put a bullet in the chamber, or that I hadn't removed it once I realized it was a doe instead of a buck.

I'd hit the doe right where I was aiming. And I felt horrible.

Walking up to the animal, I saw the doe wasn't quite dead. We made eye contact. I was not okay that I'd just done that.

What do I do now?

I didn't know what to do at all. After a few more minutes, the doe finally died. I stayed there for about half an hour, trying to figure out what to do.

Who should I tell?

Eventually, I hiked back to camp.

"I shot a doe by accident," I told the guys. "I don't want to waste the meat. We should take it back."

"Nope," said Mike, the oldest. "We'll get arrested if we take it back. It's against the law."

Emphatic agreement all around from the other boys. I felt terrible, but we left the doe where it was. No chance of getting caught; we were in the middle of nowhere. That type of legal worry wasn't what I had to wrestle with.

The experience disturbed me because I was responsible for something bad that had happened. I hadn't done it on purpose, but I felt the consequences of it on myself. Above all, I was pissed at myself. I blamed myself for screwing up.

After that, I could have said, "I'm out." I could've said, "No more hunting for me. No more messing with guns."

I didn't stop hunting, of course, but it was an important inflection moment. A memory that has always stuck with me. A rookie mistake that I had to learn from, that I had to make sure never happened again.

The practical and very important lesson I took from that experience was you *never* point a gun at anything unless you plan to kill it, whether your weapon has a bullet in it or not.

The connection I've always drawn from this rookie hunting mistake to my investment career and learning how to invest well is if you're going to lose money—if there's even a *chance* you might lose money—don't put yourself in a position where you can lose a lot of it. Especially when you're just figuring out how to invest.

That's a rookie mistake made by a lot of people who either inherit or come into money quickly. All of a sudden, they have all this money—like a rifle that weighs a ton and comes up to their chin when it's stood up straight. That day in New Mexico, I was alone on a mountain. The risks were low, comparatively speaking. People often think they need to invest their new money immediately, so it's not just sitting in a bank account. They know that other people invest, so they think they're going to have to invest theirs too. But there's no rush. It's more important to get your money invested right than to get it invested quickly.

And if you're going to make mistakes, whether as an investor, an entrepreneur, or a hunter, you need to start small, so you can build your skill and your confidence over time before you go big. The first time many novice hunters go out, they shouldn't try to put a gigantic deer on the ground. Most should just focus on shooting their first buck as soon as they get a chance. That's how they gain confidence—by doing. The next time, they can raise the bar and their expectations higher, committing to try for a buck that's a measure bigger. Building skills and confidence happens over time, one step at a time—and sometimes with the help of a great guide.

*Dave Young glassing for animals in the mountains above
Strawberry Reservoir near Heber City, Utah, fall 2015.*

DAY OF THE HUNTER

Your Guide to True Wealth

My name is Dave.

I'm a very serious trophy big game hunter.

I'm an award-winning investment advisor, business owner, and entrepreneur.

I'm a husband, father, and grandfather.

I'm the mayor of Orem, Utah.

I'm a member of the Church of Jesus Christ of Latter-day Saints.

Long ago, I performed over 250 times with my "Grand Illusion" full-stage magic show.

And in this book, I'm going to be your guide to hunting for true wealth.

After graduating from Brigham Young University in 1979 with a degree in business management, I began my career as an entrepreneur. By the mid-1980s, I had started a dozen businesses. First, I purchased a Diet Center franchise in Reno, Nevada. Over several years,

I grew that business into a total of ten franchises in Nevada, Illinois, and Michigan. But I wanted something local in Utah, so I opened a Maaco Auto Body & Painting franchise and an interior design store in Orem. In 1985, because I liked camping in the backcountry, I also helped a friend get a llama farm up and running in Payson, Utah. That's the type of entrepreneurship that I reveled in.

When I had over fifty employees in several states, life became busier and more complicated than I wanted it to be. In 1986, I sold all my businesses and decided to invest the profits. That was easier said than done. I wanted to find an investment company to invest my money as if it were their own. I wanted a company that cut unnecessary investment costs wherever possible. I wanted a proactive investment manager who would adjust my account depending on whether the markets were going up, down, or sideways. I didn't want an investment manager to passively buy an investment, hold it forever, and pray it worked out. After researching numerous investment companies, I couldn't find anyone to trust with my hard-earned money and future.

So my independent, entrepreneurial spirit kicked in again. Later that year, I established The Center for Financial Excellence and started managing my own investment accounts. After all, if you can't trust someone to do something for you, the only course of action left is to do it yourself.

I researched investment strategies designed to increase returns and reduce risk. I also developed my own investment models and believed in them so much that I invested my own life savings and started my own investment advisory firm. The vast majority of financial advisors don't make the same investments they advise their clients to make. Typically, the only skin they've got in the game is to generate revenue for themselves from their client's money.

How am I different?

I didn't set out to be a financial advisor. All I set out to do was to figure out how to manage my own money. Once I did that, I realized I could make money for other people too. I could help them. Even now,

I'm invested right alongside my clients. That's not a normal path for a financial advisor.

In October 1987, the stock market went through a severe and rapid downturn. On October 19, known as Black Monday, the S&P 500 and Dow Jones Industrial Average lost more than 20 percent of its value, the largest percentage drop in a single day up to that point in time. But thanks to the models I built, I got out of the market before the drop hit.[1] When my friends and family saw my success, they began asking me to manage their investment accounts too.

Between 1986 and 1993, the accounts I managed generated significant returns.[2] In late 1993, I registered Paragon Capital Management with the U.S. Securities and Exchange Commission (SEC) and began taking on additional clients. In 2005, Paragon Capital Management filed a DBA ("doing business as") and became known as Paragon Wealth Management.

Today, Paragon manages about $150 million for 160 households. Our methods have attracted national and local attention. I've been interviewed by *BusinessWeek*, *CNBC*, *The Wall Street Journal*, *The Deseret Morning News*, KSL Radio, and other media. I've also written articles for *Utah Valley Magazine*, *Utah Valley Business Q*, *Utah CEO Magazine*'s blog, *The Enterprise* business journal, Paragon's blog, Money Manager's Live, and others.

I've been named a Premier Advisor by the National Association of Board Certified Advisory Practices (NABCAP) five times and was honored to receive the exclusive Advisors with Heart Award, which is only given to fourteen Investment Advisors nationwide. As of 2023, Paragon has won the Best of State Award thirteen times, which recognizes the best organizations in the state that excel (in each category) in their work, use innovative methods, and help to create a better life for the people of Utah.[3] Over the past three decades, Paragon has helped

---

1 See Appendix A for disclosures.

2 See Appendix A for disclosures.

3 For full descriptions of the NABCAP and Best of State Award, see Appendix A.

charities in Utah raise close to $20 million, funds that have been used for numerous scholarships and other programs.

Community work, public service, and philanthropy are incredibly important to me. In 2010, I helped my daughters Shannon and Katie found the Live Your Dream Foundation after Katie became a single mother when her husband Byron—my son-in-law and a valued team member at Paragon—passed away unexpectedly. Our Foundation gives scholarships to single mothers in Utah, so they can get an education and provide for their families.

In 2021, I ran for mayor of Orem—a growing city of 100,000 + people—and won. I realized that I had a unique responsibility to my long-time community, and that my business experience and expertise could do good in government. I wish the politicking and personal attacks didn't come with the job, but, as with all things in life, you have to take the bad with the good. I'm happy to be able to safeguard taxpayer money and promote fiscal responsibility. My goal is to create an environment where families can thrive. That also includes guiding Orem into the future with forward-thinking policies that plan for growth while at the same time protecting the family neighborhoods and values that have made the city such a great place to live, work, and raise a family.

By sharing stories and lessons from my personal and professional life, I'll show you what it takes to hunt and bag true wealth. It's hard work and thrilling. It's the successes and the mistakes. It's totally worth it. Because you deserve to live a genuinely happy, fulfilling, and financially abundant life.

On the Hunt for My Best Trade

This is how a talking head, a half-dead deer, and a rusty pay phone helped me make some serious money.

It was early October 1998, I was forty-eight years old, and I had a week-long deer hunt planned. On a sunny Wednesday morning, I headed from Utah to a remote area in Eastern Idaho with two of my buddies, Richard King and his son, Ben. We made camp and set up so that we were ready to hit the trails on our four-wheelers early the following morning.

Life was great.

The markets were another story.

Investor sentiment was tanking. We'd been in cash since mid-August. The talking heads on TV were painting horrendous scenarios. One particularly doomsday market strategist on CNBC predicted that the Dow was going to fall from its July high of 9,400 to 6,000. If our models and systems continued to line up, I knew I'd have to move against the direction of the market and go long on the NASDAQ-100.

This far into the backcountry, my cell phone didn't get service. We passed an abandoned gas station right before the turn onto a rough dirt road. I took a mental note that it had a shabby pay phone halfway to falling apart. For four days in a row, I hunted during the morning, then drove my four-wheeler fifteen miles to that pay phone so I could call the office by 11:00 a.m. Every day, my assistants, Doreen and Melissa, relayed key market numbers to me. Then I'd graph them by hand on a piece of paper. This handwritten chart gave me the information I needed to decide whether to take a position or not.

Several weeks before, our indicators had taken us completely out of the market, so we were sitting on *a lot* of cash. Doreen and Melissa were incredibly stressed taking directions from me long distance by way of an unreliable pay phone. They'd executed trades before, but I'd always been there to check everything before pulling the trigger. They also knew if we made a move, it would be a big, single block trade, which was unusual for us. Our trades were typically more diversified, made up of six to ten large, diversified positions. But I was putting together a trade that would go 100 percent into the NASDAQ-100, all in one shot.

On the morning of October 8, 1998, before dawn, we headed to an area I wanted to hunt. Once it was light, I immediately spotted a really nice buck. I quietly slid off my four-wheeler, made sure I had a solid rest, took aim, and fired a single shot. The buck went down.

This is too easy, I thought. *This is not my life. It must be a sign.*

All I could think about next was getting back to that pay phone before 11:00 a.m. I hurried over to take care of the deer, and...he was gone. The buck had crawled away out of my sight and taken off down the mountain in the direction of a nearby river.

So down the mountain we went—losing almost 2,000 frickin' feet in elevation! An hour and a half later, I was able to take a second shot that ended our race together. The buck dropped in the middle of the river. He really was a good buck, and I knew I'd celebrate later.

In the meantime, I told my friend Ben that he was going to have to clean the deer out because I had to get back to the pay phone and make that call. I left my gun and pack with Ben, then climbed and hiked about two miles, as fast as I could, criss-crossing back and forth up the mountain, and then across the top. Getting on my four-wheeler, I drove forty-five minutes to the gas station on gnarly dirt roads.

All the while, I was thinking, *Is that stupid pay phone even going to work? I hope I have enough quarters!*

We were at 100 percent cash, and if I didn't get that trade in, I knew I would miss my window of opportunity.

After making it to the gas station, I called the office. The technical indicators lined up perfectly. I pulled the trigger. Melissa and Doreen did their jobs perfectly.

Had I waited even an hour more, I would have missed the trade. Timing is everything. Calculated risk is everything. The greater the risk, the greater the potential reward. But you have to know what you're doing. You need experience, skill, the right equipment, and support.

We swung from 100 percent cash to 100 percent invested on October 8. Over the next two trading days, the NASDAQ-100 gained 10 percent. By the beginning of February 1999, four months later, the trade had gone up 88 percent, almost doubling our multimillion-dollar investment.[4]

Quite a successful week—big bucks were made . . . and taken.

What It Means to Be Truly Wealthy

When I was younger, I thought money was freedom and happiness.

The assumption that more money will make us happier is etched into our collective consciousness. It's so basic that most people never

---

4 See Appendix A for disclosures.

stop to question it. Happiness is something we all want; it's the holy grail of Western civilization. Our culture champions it, promotes it with billions of dollars in advertising each year, and institutionalizes it in our public policy. Happiness is also the primary promise that most good investment advisors focus on.

Everything we do, consciously or unconsciously, we do because we believe or hope that it will make us happy. In many ways, we do have a lot to be happy about. The average American now lives much better than most kings and queens have throughout history. American purchasing power is higher than ever. Homes, cars, technology, and entertainment are everywhere. So, is the assumption true? Are we happier?

No!

The spectacular increase in American wealth and consumerism has had almost no net positive effect on our society's overall happiness. Plenty of studies now show that believing money is more important than other values—like relationships with loved ones, spirituality, and service to others—is actually detrimental to happiness. Clearly, there's more to happiness than wealth, luxury, and material comforts.

Here's a fun question then: How much money do we need to maximize our happiness?

The bottom line is that financial security remains the gold standard. Reaching a solid middle-class income is harder than it's ever been for many Americans. But once your household income reaches that middle-class range, increased income can, instead, have a diminishing positive impact on your happiness and well-being.

Getting rich simply doesn't guarantee your happiness.[5] Depending on the price you pay to earn that wealth, more income can even reduce your quality of life. Struggles with loneliness, self-esteem, and mental health are rampant, regardless of how big your bank account is. As the late Ed Diener—psychologist, professor, and author—rightly said,

---

5 Chris Taylor, "What the World's Longest Happiness Study Says about Money," *Reuters*, February 6, 2023, https://www.reuters.com/markets/wealth/what-worlds-longest-happiness-study-says-about-money-2023-02-06/, accessed June 15, 2023.

"Materialism is toxic for happiness."[6] But most Americans don't seem to believe this, and instead, they fill their lives with things that won't help them get where they want to be.

Why do we chase money so hard? Part of it is America's culture, of course. The media and advertising industries are two giant institutions that have a vested interest in ensuring we consume more and more *stuff* each year. But another part of the problem is a more subtle villain: human nature.

Humans tend to return to a stable state of happiness (or unhappiness) no matter what positive or negative experiences we go through. Psychologists call this the "hedonic treadmill." As our income increases or we buy fancy new things, our expectations about what and how much we're supposed to have also rise proportionally. We adapt to our new materialistic normal and after a while no longer feel any permanent gain in happiness. To maintain the same level of happiness through consumption, then, we have to continually buy new things. This is what the concept of retail therapy is all about. It's great for the economy but bad for you and your financial security.

As an investment advisor, I often work with people who believe that more money will buy them more happiness. For decades I've watched investors, clients, and people I care about try and fail to make this belief a reality—because it's simply not true. Every year, I've gotten better and better at helping them make money.[7] And every year, my drive to help people figure out what would really, genuinely make them happy has grown.

That's what I set out to do in this book. Once you understand what will bring you real happiness, you can determine how much money you actually need to live your ideal life. It may be a lot less than you originally thought.

---

6 Marilyn Elias, "Psychologists Now Know What Makes People Happy," *USA TODAY*, December 8, 2002, https://www.tamdistrict.org/cms/lib8/CA01000875/Centricity/Domain/576/what_makes_people_happy.pdf, accessed July 6, 2023.

7 See Appendix A for disclosures.

Hunting for True Wealth is not only about making money. You will learn how to build financial wealth. Along the way, though, you'll discover something more important: You'll discover what it means to be truly wealthy.

- True wealth is the lifelong experience of deep happiness, fulfillment, and learning.

- True wealth is focusing on the overall quality of your life.

- True wealth is becoming an empathetic, caring person.

- True wealth is owning your life and taking back control of your life when it's gone sideways.

True wealth isn't an achievement or prize you win once you reach a certain age or once your bank account gets big enough. It's the sum total of all your experiences, good and bad, at any given point in your life. Getting that sum total right is the very essence of true wealth.

We all experience trials, stumbles, and losses in life. You can learn and grow from them, or you can let them diminish and trap you in a state of being that you don't deserve or want. Because we all have different experiences, everyone's version of true wealth will differ slightly. My job is to show you the values and principles of true wealth that you can use as lessons, signposts, and goals.

My ultimate goal—for me and for you—is to experience true wealth, not just monetary wealth. Achieving financial security is best thought of as one important part of figuring out, over the course of all your life experiences, what true wealth is for you, why it matters more than money, and how you can shift your focus and efforts to building it.

So I challenge you, right here and now, to ask yourself two questions:

- "What do I want my life to look like?"

- "Does my life look like that right now?"

If it doesn't, you can pivot and change. You can invest in yourself. You can take your life back. I've had to do this multiple times throughout my life. It's what I'm working on again right now—getting my own life back.

To ask these questions of yourself, you don't need to have a lot of money. All you need is the willingness to take a step back and think intentionally about where you want to go. The alternative is just letting the wind blow you wherever it takes you. Letting yourself be carried along is easier than imagining the life you want, setting goals, and planning out the steps that will create that life for you.

Easy is boring. Easy is a trap. Easy makes you weak.

Hunting for true wealth isn't easy. But living a full, adventurous life with intention will always be better than just letting life happen to you. True wealth is for everyone, no matter your age, career, or life experience. That means this book is for you.

You may be young and ambitious, want to build wealth, but don't want to figure everything out for yourself. You may be a lifelong professional entrepreneur who wants to start your first, third, or fifth company. You may have entered the overwhelming "sandwich years," that period in your life when you're taking care of both children and parents. You may be in your sixties and feeling the urgency to figure out your game plan for retirement (or semi-retirement) as soon as possible. You may have come into wealth quickly (e.g., children who have inherited wealth, lottery winners, professional athletes). You may be a big game hunter who wants to live the way you play.

This book is for you.

Thirteen Values to Live By

"Thirteen" is a very important number in my life. It's come up over and over again, framing and shaping my experiences in big and small ways. Not surprisingly, when I set out to list the values that I live my life by, the number came to thirteen. These are the values I've actively strived to live by, model for others, and teach my children. They are also the values to live by to find true wealth. They're based on the premise that every single person on this earth walks the same path. We are born, we live—that's our life experience, who we are and who we become—and then we die and move onto what comes next. The values you live by directly impact the quality and direction of your life.

Three Types of Wealth

1. Monetary wealth refers to the financial assets and resources that you possess. It represents the value of your financial holdings, including cash, bank accounts, investments, real estate, and other tangible and intangible assets that have a monetary value. Monetary wealth is typically measured in terms of a person's net worth, which is calculated by subtracting liabilities, such as debts or obligations, from the total value of their assets. Most people only think about and pay attention to building monetary wealth.

Two subtypes of monetary wealth are **inherited wealth** and **retirement wealth**. Inherited wealth refers to financial assets and resources that you receive through inheritance. Retirement wealth refers to financial assets and resources that you accumulate through your working years to support your retirement. Both subtypes of wealth often involve coming into large sums of money abruptly. Whether or not you know it's coming, gaining access to a large family inheritance or 401(k) that has $1.5 million bucks in it can feel sudden. In both cases, the pressure of that big jump in your wealth can get overwhelming quickly and turn into an immediate problem you need to solve. If you don't manage that serious amount of money correctly, the risk that you'll lose it is high.

2. Self-serving wealth refers to the creation and use of financial assets and resources primarily for your own benefit and self-interest. It involves a mindset or approach where you prioritize personal gain and work to maximize your own wealth without considering the well-being or needs of others. People who focus on building self-serving wealth often place a high value on luxury possessions and high social status. They are more likely to disregard broader social responsibilities, the importance of community, and ethical considerations. Self-serving wealth can also

(continues on next page)

arise when financially wealthy people trap themselves in a frugal box—also known as a scarcity or poverty mindset—and refuse or become unable to spend the money they have to experience deep happiness, fulfillment, and learning (more on this in chapter 10).

3. True wealth refers to the lifelong, net experience of deep happiness, fulfillment, and learning. You need the freedom and opportunity that financial security provides to be truly wealthy, but monetary wealth doesn't guarantee you will find true wealth.

Throughout the chapters that follow, you'll see these thirteen values woven into both my hunting stories and the lessons I share. Adopting these values in your own life can help guide the choices you make and the path you take to true wealth. They can also motivate you to stop wasting time and go get the life you want.

1. Adventure

Adventure is not only for the adrenaline junkies of the world. Adventure, at its core, is change. It is stress. It is growth. It is doing new things, pushing yourself out of your comfort zone, and going new places—especially where no one else has been before. A spirit of adventure crystallizes the unique and special differences you bring into this world.

2. Living in Alignment

To be truly happy, your life must be aligned. Essential to alignment is incorporating the experiences and lessons that you learned in each of your previous life stages—childhood, youth, early adulthood, and onward—and became the fabric of who you are as a unique individual. Living in alignment means recognizing, accepting, and leaning into the foundational principles of who you are as a person. It means being true to yourself.

When you're out of alignment, you lie in bed at night believing in your heart and soul that *this is who I am.* Day by day, however, a different version of you is walking around. Your behaviors and actions aren't in alignment with your identity. Your beliefs and values don't match how you are living your life, often because of external pressures from other people, circumstances, and conditions. I firmly believe that addiction and substance abuse stem from this type of misalignment.

3. Family

Family is core to who we all are. That's not easy. The people closest to you don't always make good decisions. They struggle, and that, in turn, affects you. But they are still your core, and they affect your life from beginning to end. It's impossible to achieve true wealth by denying the truth of your family, whatever that truth may be for you.

4. Fitness and Health

Society has moved so far away from the natural food chain. Yet, or perhaps as a result, fitness and health have only become more closely tied to happiness. Life expectancy is longer than ever before, which means that poor health will affect you for longer than ever too. Without fitness and health, you'll only ever be a passive observer of adventure rather than an active participant.

5. Freedom

Freedom is living your life the way you want to, not how anyone else thinks you should. It's finding purpose and having the time and financial security for recreational activities that make you happy. Freedom is earned through hard work; it should be fought for and never taken for granted.

6. Gratitude

Without gratitude, you'll never truly be wealthy. It doesn't matter how much money you accumulate. If you aren't grateful for what you have, then what you have will never be enough, and it will never have the value you want it to have.

Gratitude colors both your view of the world and your own life. It's very difficult to be angry, bitter, or negative when your mindset is focused on appreciating what you have and who you get to share it with. Those are opposing forces. They are oil and water. And gratitude is stronger. It has the power to push the negativity and bad parts of life out.

7. Honesty

Without having foundational honesty in all that you do, you're living a lie. Until you dig down to that foundation of honesty, you cannot have true conversations with yourself or with the people around you. True wealth will remain out of reach because you won't truly know yourself, the reality of your life, and the possibilities that your life holds.

8. Listening and Learning to Listen

Every single person in this world wants to be heard. They have a story to tell. And, so often, so many of us don't get heard. Society has been built on barriers, selfishness, and the absence of foundational honesty. Listening and learning to listen allows you to be involved in other people's lives, to overcome the barriers that separate us, and to expand your impact beyond yourself.

9. Love

Love encompasses all the facets of your life that give you meaning and make you feel happy: love for people, for animals, for relationships that add to your life rather than take away from it. Love is connection and the goodness that you and everyone else deserves.

10. Optimism

Pessimism is the true enemy of progress, success, and happiness. So many people today say *it won't work; it can't happen; this isn't possible.* It is. Just make it happen. True wealth is rooted in optimism.

11. Spirituality

Spirituality is belief in a higher power, whatever that higher power is for and to you. From spirituality comes the recognition that there is more to your life than just the person who exists in the here and now. If you can embrace the spiritual side of life, then you have access to the essence of true wealth.

12. Born Ready

People always ask me, "Are you ready?"

Whether my wife and I are going to a store we've been to dozens of times before, or I'm leaving on a once-in-a-lifetime hunting trip, my answer is always the same: "I was born ready."

Born ready is about welcoming whatever the world has to throw at you. Don't shrink from that. Don't diminish yourself or anything that makes up part of your life. Live every day like you were *born ready,* and you'll find the empowerment you need to chase true wealth.

When I was a much younger man, a bigwig from New York named Jack tried to recruit me to work for his company selling investments. I knew a little bit about his investments and company, but not enough to say I was in a position to talk about them with any confidence. We met in the lobby of a skyscraper, shook hands, and got onto an elevator that took us to a large company boardroom on the twenty-fifth floor.

On the way up, Jack said, "I want you to do my board presentation today on this."

At that point, I hadn't even been hired.

What the hell? "You want me to present to a conference room of fifteen board members?" I asked. "I don't even know this stuff."

"You know more than they do," Jack said. "I just want to see what you can do."

That was a *born ready* moment. I did the presentation. We got the account. I was willing to jump into the fray and make it happen.

13. Vision

You need to have a proactive picture of where you're going with your life. Without a vision, life just happens to you. You'll end up wherever the wind blows you, instead of where you want to be. True wealth comes from envisioning it, then going out and getting it.

The Five Principles of True Wealth

This book will help you understand and embrace the power of true wealth. It'll be fun, informative, and personal. You'll read entertaining big game hunting stories, learn how to invest your money the right way, and discover what you need to know for your own pursuit of that more enriching experience of true wealth. I'm incredibly excited to share that wealth with you.

The upcoming chapters of this book alternate between hunting stories (Chapters 1, 3, 5, 7, and 9) and lessons about building both financial and true wealth (Chapters 2, 4, 6, 8, and 10). I take you to Zimbabwe, Alaska, Northern British Columbia, Idaho, Utah, New Mexico, and more. I hunt leopard, bear, mountain goat, mule and whitetail deer, elk, and antelope. There's a story about catching poachers, another about whitewater rafting in the Grand Canyon, and another about bungee jumping in New Zealand. (That last story is about my son, Shawn!)

Because so many useful parallels can be drawn between big game hunting, financial investing, and finding true wealth, I weave more stories into the lesson chapters and use all the chapters to explain and illustrate what I've boiled down to become The Five Principles of True Wealth.

The Five Principles of True Wealth

1. Go big or go home.
2. Build solid relationships; value your family, friends, and community.
3. Don't panic; things go wrong.
4. Expect bear markets; be positioned for bull markets.
5. Live your legacy.

These are the five principles that will lead you to deep happiness and success. They are your learning path. Following these five principles will ensure you get the sum total of your experiences in this life right. They are the cumulative value of a life well lived and a truly wealthy person. As I guide you through these principles, I'll share expertise, advice, and wisdom I've gained across all my different roles in life: investment advisor, business owner, entrepreneur, family man, mayor, big game hunter, and more.

Here's a quick summary of what you'll get in the lesson chapters:

Chapter 2 introduces you to the seven steps you need to put into practice to build your financial wealth. An important part of investing and growing your money is understanding the importance of risk tolerance, increasing your odds, and keeping your options open.

Chapter 4 shows you how vital solid relationships are to true wealth, and what it means to truly value all the different types of people in your life. After reading it, I invite you to imagine writing your own chapter about the various relationships in your life. How much wealth would your chapter reveal?

Chapter 6 explores four ways to develop the skill of remaining calm, steady, and in control when life hits you hard and fast. By learning from your mistakes, listening to your inner guide, chasing your edge, and finding reminders to be grateful, you can keep panic out of your life.

Chapter 8 explains what bear and bull markets are in the context of financial markets and your personal life, and how you can navigate, survive, and thrive through them. To do this, I bring together the tool-box of fundamentals you need to learn and practice. Keep an eye out for these fundamentals throughout the entire book, as I introduce and build on them throughout all the chapters.

Chapter 10 helps you rethink your legacy. We all want a legacy, but not many of us realize we can have one *now*. It's entirely possible to live your legacy in the present by spending your money, doing the right thing for the right reason, and giving back.

Together we'll cover a lot in this book. I know what I'm sharing here has helped me find more true wealth, and it will help make you wealthier too, in all the ways that matter most. I like to get straight to the point—so let's get to it.

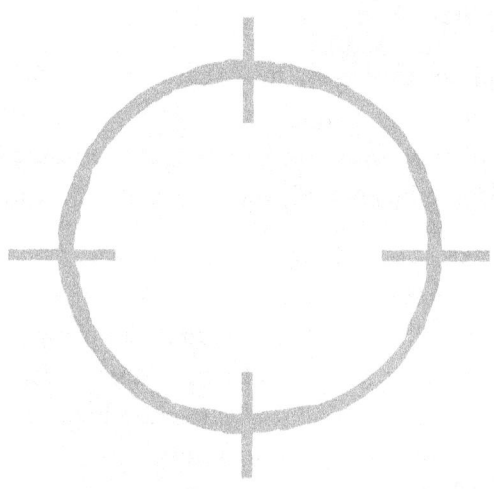

CHAPTER 1

HUNTING LEOPARD
IN ZIMBABWE

I've always been obsessed with leopards. They're really difficult to locate and kill and, in my opinion, probably the most ferocious animal in Africa. If you want to hunt a leopard, you can expect the hunt to take a couple of weeks, and you'll have about a 15 to 20 percent chance of success. That's very low. Most hunters who go to Africa will bag half a dozen to a dozen animals, but not a leopard. It's too much time and effort.

In 2002, I asked my son, Shawn, where he wanted to go for his high school senior trip. Like me, he's always been all about hunting, so he picked Africa. Zimbabwe has the biggest leopards in the world, so that's where we decided to go. At the time, however, Zimbabwe was extremely dangerous for tourists because of civil unrest and conflict stemming from President Robert Mugabe's redistribution of land controlled by white farmers to landless black Zimbabweans.

Despite these challenges, I forged ahead, contacting Jacob Tshuma, a renowned big game hunter who operated a successful outfitting guide business in Zimbabwe. After a lot of planning, we got everything booked. Shawn and I were scheduled to fly into Harare, the capital city of Zimbabwe. But about two and a half weeks before leaving, we got notice that the circumstances were simply too dangerous.

"Jacob's been arrested and thrown in jail on political charges," his wife told me by phone. Over time, I learned her husband never came out of that jail, and I was never able to find out exactly what had happened.

I connected with Michael, a friend of Jacob's, who said he could be our guide instead and take us out on the hunt. Was I really going to take my son to a mess of a country, though?

"Let's do it," Shawn kept insisting. "Let's do it."

Because we already had our plane tickets and other travel expenses locked in, I decided to go ahead with the trip despite the sketchy situation. Shawn was very excited.

Because of all the rioting, we flew into Bulawayo instead of Harare.

Michael met us at the airport in an old beater bomber Nissan truck. In the bed of the pickup sat a fifty-gallon gas tank—picture a metal drum with a sealed top—and an armed guard protecting it from being stolen because of rampant fuel shortages. We drove by gas stations with dozens, sometimes hundreds, of cars lined up that had all been abandoned because drivers had run out of gas and were unable to fill up again.

Immediately, I thought, *This is crazy!* We'd been told Michael would be picking us up in a Range Rover, not a Nissan. Michael was a happy-go-lucky white South African. As soon as he jumped out of the Nissan to greet us, we trusted him. He also seemed at home with the chaos of the country surrounding us.

"Four days ago, I was at a stoplight," he explained. "And a mob rushed my car. They pulled me out of the Rover and took it." He never saw the Range Rover again, but luckily, he wasn't injured except for some scrapes and bruises.

Keeping a low profile, we left the airport. Once Michael got us away from the traffic, we flew down the road in this broken-down Nissan with this exorbitant amount of gas. Everywhere we went, Michael and his guard told us to hide, to duck down and stay out of sight.

As we passed villages and open terrain, one of the first buildings we saw that looked at all modern—high-tech, even—was a huge industrial plant.

"What's that?" I asked Michael.

"The asbestos plant," he replied. Not so modern then! At the time, African countries still used asbestos in all their building materials, even though it had been banned everywhere else.

Whenever we got close to a city, we'd have to pass blockades, checkpoints, and guards. Everyone carried machetes. When we had to refill the pickup with gas, we stopped on the side of the road. The first time, Michael and the guard began futzing with the storage drum in the back.

I was shocked when the guard took out a hammer and began whacking away at the drum's sealed top. "What the hell are you doing?"

"Oh," said Michael reasonably. "We just have to get the top off."

"Yeah, but one spark will blow us to kingdom come."

"It'll be fine." Michael wasn't the least bit worried. I took Shawn about a hundred yards away to wait.

This is insane, I thought.

So the journey felt a bit nerve-wracking, although I was very excited about the hunt. I figured we'd be fine and feel more comfortable as soon as we got away from civilization. I've never been much of a second-guesser; once we were in Zimbabwe, I accepted the hand we were dealt and went along for the ride. Meanwhile, Shawn was having the time of his life. He's very much a go-big or go-home kind of kid.

As we got closer to our hunting area, Michael said, "You can't wear camo out here. People will think you're working for the government. And if we see *anyone* while we're out hunting leopard, shoot them."

Um, what? "I'm not shooting any people."

"They're poachers. If they get caught poaching, it's punishable by death. That means if they come across us, they might think we're going to turn them in." Michael shrugged. "We've got to shoot them before they shoot us."

I shook my head. I couldn't believe we were having this conversation. "If they start shooting, I'll shoot back. But I'm not going to randomly start shooting people."

We set up camp a little way back from a muddy, slow-moving river. Drinking from it was a big no. Vegetation surrounded us; we were definitely in an African jungle. Every single plant had thorns and stickers. There's so much wildlife in Africa; that's the only way plants would survive. The temperature got up around 80 degrees during the day, so not terribly hot, and it would cool off pretty good at night. This wasn't the lush green jungle many associate with Africa. We were in the African savanna, where it's more brown than green, like the desert of Mexico. We had to make our way through thick patches of sticker plants below baobab trees with deep roots systems that prevent the soil from eroding.

Beside our camp was a former bridge, which we would have had to cross to get to the hunting areas on the other side of the river. But, like everything on this trip, a month before we arrived there'd been a once-in-a-century flood that had taken out the bridge, as well as another bridge farther down the river. Getting around the river taking a different route became a three-hour trip for us each way.

The only other choice would be to cross the river by foot, which was about ten-to twelve-feet deep. We would need to cross it by jumping from one protruding rock to another. That wouldn't be a problem. The problem was the wildlife. Crocodiles sunbathed on boulders that dotted the river; hippos milled about farther downstream. Hippos, in particular, are very territorial and the number one killer in Africa. They'll scream at you and charge. They terrified us more than the crocodiles. In that area, there were eight to ten hippos.

On the first day of our hunt, Shawn, Michael, and I snuck down to the river with our gear, keeping crouched down in the brush and bushes. We began hopping across the slippery rocks. As soon as the hippos caught sight of us, their mouths gaped wide open, showing their huge tusks and teeth. As they moved toward us, they started screaming, getting as close to us as ten yards away.

Time to move! Shawn fell in the water a couple times, but he was very quick getting back up onto the rocks. We made it across and hurried out of sight of the river. The hippos didn't get close enough to stop us this time.

Our hunting party wasn't only just me, Shawn, and Michael. Once we got to the hunting areas, we were joined by a younger assistant guide, another guide who brought several tracking dogs and three incredible local trackers. Unlike us, they all went around the river instead of crossing it.

That first day, we shot several impalas and a zebra. Then we tied these bait animals up in trees near where our trackers thought leopards were likely to frequent, based on the tracks they found and what they already knew about leopard territory in the area. Lastly, we raked all around the trees, erasing any evidence of our passage.

After leaving the bait animals overnight in the trees, we returned to camp. Luckily, none of us got taken out by a crocodile or hippo!

Before sunup the next day, we returned to the strung-up animals. The goal was to find a fresh leopard track, put the dogs on its scent, and follow them. More specifically, we were looking for a big male track.

For five days, we followed this routine—and never found the track we wanted. We saw smaller male and female leopards, but never that giant trophy leopard.

On the sixth day, we finally got one. A huge male track.

We set the dogs loose. Most of them were bluetick hounds, a valuable breed from the USA that bays as they chase a scent. But one little terrier with an attitude also hunted with the pack and only barked if it actually saw the leopard.

We all took off behind the dogs, listening for the terrier's bark. For three and a half miles, they led us through the dense savanna, across the river, and over hills. At the top of a hill, we heard the terrier begin to bark. At the bottom of the hill, we saw another river, and on the other side of it, I finally saw what we'd traveled so far for: a leopard.

The leopard had clawed its way up into the top of a tree and saw us at the same time we saw it, even though we were about 300 yards away. Slowly, we made our way down the hill. Tall grass and a wood cave like a beaver dam surrounded the base of the tree beside the river.

The five dogs were all going nuts baying. The leopard was going nuts. We could barely hear. Then the leopard roared—an incredible sound that made the hair on the back of your neck stand up. Leopards have different vocal cords than cougars; the sound a leopard makes is more like a lion's roar.

We made it down the hill to the bank of the river. After losing sight of the leopard in the tall grass, we saw the big cat had dropped down to the beaver dam structure. We waited for it to go back up the tree, which would give me a clear, easy shot—no problem.

But the leopard didn't go back up the tree. Instead, it started a vicious fight with the dogs that would go on for over an hour. Every couple minutes, a dog would fly through the air above the tall grass, crying from getting whacked by the leopard. "Do something!" the dogs' owner yelled, worried for the lives of his expensive dogs, urging us to hurry up and end the mayhem.

We were in the thick of it. We couldn't retreat. We had no options at this point. Either the leopard was going to die, or the dogs were. The only decision we could make was to cross the river so we could get eyes on the leopard. Petrified, the local trackers were not okay with this plan. Their eyes looked as big as saucers. They'd seen the type of damage this animal could do.

After deciding we had to cross the river, I told Shawn, "Your job is to stay over here and video what happens." He didn't argue. The dog owner stayed with my son, while the rest of us crossed the river, which was muddy and slow-moving.

At the edge of the river a little way down from the fighting animals, we noticed something that looked like a big log. When we got to the middle of the river, though, the log stood up—a crocodile. At the sight of the croc sliding into the water toward us, we all turned around and hightailed it back the way we'd come. It was all asses and elbows. No one wanted to be last out. Safely out of the water again, we still had to do something about the battle to the death going on. The dogs' barking and roar of the leopard still sounded unbelievable.

The crocodile owned that part of the river. Hiking along the bank, we searched for somewhere else that might be safer to cross. About 300 to 400 yards upstream, the river narrowed slightly, out of sight of the crocodile. We crossed and came back down the other side toward the dogs and leopard.

"Get your gun ready," Michael said when we'd gotten about fifty yards from the fight. "Make sure it's loaded. Get that safety off. You need to be able to shoot without a second's notice." He and his assistant guide also readied their guns.

The closer we got, the louder the noise became. This was intense.

Forty yards. "No shot," I said. The leopard was down in the grass, and the dogs were right there with it, so we had to be careful not to shoot them.

"We've got to keep going," Michael urged us. "We've got to get closer until someone gets a shot."

The rule was that you never get closer than more than thirty yards to a leopard. They're too fast. Now that we were at thirty yards, Michael added, "It's going to jump on one of us. That's just the way this works. It'll jump on whoever makes eye contact with it."

The plan was simple, if nuts. The person who got jumped would fall to the ground, flat on their stomach to protect their vitals, and put their hands over the back of their neck. The other two of us would shoot the leopard off the person on the ground.

This situation was no longer about my hunt. Whoever could get the shot had to take it to end the chaos.

Twenty yards. Ten yards. All three of us were totally focused.

Finally, I saw the leopard in the grass and made eye contact. It immediately jumped straight toward me. I didn't even have time to get my gun up to my shoulder. I just hipshot it, and it fell dead at my feet.

Everything went from chaos to silence, just like that.

Without really aiming, I stepped to the right, pulled the trigger, and hit the leopard in the vitals. Pure instinct and reaction. We all took a breath. I discovered later that Shawn had gotten so caught up with the hunt that he forgot to turn on the video recorder.

Two of the dogs suffered big gashes and had to be bandaged up. I don't know if they survived. It turned out that, while the dogs were tracking our huge male, a female leopard had crossed its tracks. Female leopards have more powerful scents than males, so the dogs had veered off on its trail instead. We didn't realize until it was dead that we'd gotten the female, not the big male.

Either way, everyone was very excited, relieved, and hopped up on adrenaline. We got the leopard rigged up on some poles fashioned from tree branches and carried it back to the vehicles. After that, we made our way to the village where the three trackers lived. Whenever we drove by any locals, they'd see the leopard and start cheering. It was like winning the Super Bowl because leopards were such a danger to them—especially to their small kids and animals.

That night, in the middle of somewhere in Zimbabwe, the village put on a celebration. Dancing, drumming, and drinking. The locals took turns holding the leopard up and cheering. Everyone was very happy, so everything we'd been through—it was worth it.

But even that celebration wasn't the end. After the leopard hunt, Shawn and I traveled from Zimbabwe to Victoria Falls, one of the seven natural wonders of the world with spectacular waterfalls. We decided we *had* to raft the Zambezi River below. With level V and VI rapids on a scale of VI, it's known as one of the most difficult stretches of river ever. Adding to the crazy, the Zambezi has crocodiles up to eighteen feet swimming its waters and lounging on the banks. Knowing you're likely getting thrown out of the raft, the presence of huge crocs adds another dimension of danger.

At one point on our rafting excursion, we hit a major rapid, and our raft shot straight up in the air, throwing us all out. As I came back out of the water, the raft came down and nailed me right in the head, torquing my neck. It hurt so bad, I had to go get my neck fixed. So I went into what you *might* call a "town," found what you *might* call a "doctor," and then lay down on the doctor's table spotted with blood and dirt. I was only willing to do that because my neck hurt so bad. The doctor gave my neck a super deep massage, and when I left, my neck felt great! It didn't make sense. I had no idea how he made that happen.

Shawn and I then went across the border to Zambia where we each flew a device like a paraglider with a prop that looked like a lawn mower engine. We both flew right in front of the falls—another spectacular view and another extremely sketch experience, making this hunting trip in Zimbabwe the most incredible father-son senior trip ever!

CHAPTER 2

GO BIG OR GO HOME

M y son Shawn has an amazing "go big or go home" approach to life.

As a child, Shawn loved to freestyle ski, the most extreme type of skiing. It includes flips, spins, moguls, half-pipe, and slopestyle skiing.

At the ripe young age of eleven years old, Shawn was on the Snowboard Freestyle Team and later the Wasatch Freestyle Ski Team that included Snowbird and Deer Valley. One day, he asked me if he could go train in New Zealand. Not crazy about sending my kid halfway around the world by himself, I told Shawn, "Hey, if you want to earn the money and pay for half, then I'll pay the other half."

The six-week program didn't come cheap. Shawn would train with top-tier skiers, who would go on to compete and medal in the Olympics. But I underestimated my own kid, thinking he wouldn't be able to earn enough money. Sure enough, Shawn went out and did a bunch of odd jobs, then sold some of his stuff to boot. After all this conniving to scrimp and scrounge, lo and behold, he came up with half the money.

Well, I had to keep my end of the deal.

We set up the trip and off went eleven-year-old Shawn to New Zealand. He had no fear about going and even forgot to call us when he arrived. This big adventure took place before everyone had a cell phone, so we didn't hear from our eleven-year-old for almost two full days. After that, Cathy and I got very few updates from him about what he was doing.

Almost halfway through the trip, Shawn called me and asked, "Hey, Dad, you don't care if I go skydiving, do you?"

"You are not going skydiving," I said. "That's insane." We had a big debate, and thankfully I ended up nixing that idea.

Instead, Shawn decided—without my input—to go bungee jumping.

If you're not familiar with it, bungee jumping involves throwing yourself headfirst off a platform with a lifesaving bungee cord tied around your ankles. It's not for the faint-hearted. It's for thrill-seekers, plain and simple.

Shawn, being Shawn, didn't choose just any bungee jump. He had to go for the 440-foot Nevis Bungy Jump out in the middle of nowhere. It's ranked as the second highest bungee jump in the Southern Hemisphere. Even the Jeep ride to get there was like taking your life in your own hands.

Go figure, once he got there, Shawn discovered he was too small to do the jump. His only option was to convince one of the bungee operators to do it with him. Strapped in together, the bungee would have enough weight to make it all the way down and back up.

Needless to say, Shawn made the jump.

The First Principle of True Wealth

By its very nature, hunting for true wealth is a thrill. *Hunting* means testing yourself, pushing yourself, and getting out of your comfort zone. You can't hunt if you play it safe or stay home. To find true wealth, you have to see the world for the adventure it is. You have to see *life* as an adventure.

Most people don't do this. Most people choose the easy path.

The easy path, the path of least resistance, may feel like the wisest choice you can make. It may feel like the fastest and most direct path you can take to success—at work, in your finances, or in your relationships, for example. After all, getting from point A to point B in a straight line, with no obstacles, delays, or detours, must be a sign of a smart person or a life well lived, right?

Wrong.

Without struggle, without risk, without mistakes, without stretching, you will never find true wealth. Everyone's risk tolerance is different, and you don't have to go bungee jumping to experience true wealth. But you do have to *go big* in whatever way best fits your personality.

While going big will look different for everyone, the core of this first principle for hunting true wealth and deep happiness does stay the same no matter your life experience. Going big means *taking action*. You have to actually *do it*. Going big is the opposite of "talking big."

Anyone can talk big. Only the truly wealthy stop talking and actually make it happen.

In Chapter 1, I went *big*.

Like bungee jumping, traveling to Africa and hunting leopard is not for the faint of heart. That entire trip embodies what it means to go big or go home. On the most practical of levels, I had to be physically fit and healthy. Beyond that, it required taking a risk that most hunters will turn away from. Mental toughness, commitment, and patience to endure and thrive in extreme risk all come from training. I trained myself, through hundreds of hours of practice and experience, to be the type of big game hunter who could not only face down literal life or death, but also *enjoy* the chaotic, wild ride from beginning to end. It came with unforeseen circumstances, unexpected stress, and a roller coaster of emotions. I had to stay calm even when the situation became scary or sobering. I had to commit to my objectives and do whatever it took to achieve them. And I made sure I had a guide who was also well trained, knew the lay of the land, and was worth my trust.

In this chapter, you're going to see these same themes—but in the context of investing your money. I give you seven essential steps that will help you build *financial* wealth. As you read in the introduction to this book, the assumption that the more money we have, the happier we'll be is just plain wrong. You'll also notice in the introduction that money is not one of the thirteen values of true wealth. But successfully investing it is still very, very important.

Just as physical health and fitness are prerequisites to hunting big game animals, knowing how to invest and grow your money is a prerequisite that provides you the freedom to pursue true wealth. Whether you're an entrepreneur or ambitious young adult, a caregiver to children and/or aging parents, or someone who has come into financial wealth quickly, these are the financial investment steps that will allow you to build financial wealth and speed up your hunt for true wealth.

7 Steps for Building Financial Wealth

For more than thirty-seven years, I've been helping people invest their money the right way, so they can have the freedom to live the way they want.

Many people believe that accumulating financial wealth is a random event or that, ultimately, those who become wealthy get where they are through pure luck. While it's true that some people win the lottery or receive a family inheritance, that type of sudden wealth is usually temporary if a proper investment plan isn't put in place.

To build financial wealth, you have to follow certain steps. To *keep* wealth, you have to follow those same steps. If you don't learn the steps or don't have the discipline to follow them, you won't be able to build or sustain wealth.

Here are the seven steps I recommend to build financial wealth:

1. Start now.
2. Spend less than you earn.
3. Hire a competent financial advisor.
4. Avoid unnecessary debt.
5. Avoid large losses.
6. Follow a sound, long-term strategy.
7. Be patient.

Step 1: Start now.

Don't wait another day to start saving your money. However much money you have today, right now, *that* is your starting point. There's no time to waste. By waiting, you're losing money that otherwise would be yours.

For compound interest to be truly powerful, it must have the benefit of time. The more time, the better. Think of it like a snowball rolling down a hill. It starts out small and then gets bigger the longer it rolls.

Compare two young investors who each put away $2,000 a year and earn 10 percent annually. The first investor starts at age nineteen and puts away $2,000 per year for eight years in a row and then holds it there. The second investor waits eight years before investing $2,000 per year for thirty-eight years. At the end of the thirty-eight years, the first investor's account will have grown to $941,054. The second investor's account will be at $800,896. The first investor invested $60,000 less but ended up with $140,158 more.

If you read this example and you aren't nineteen years old, don't be discouraged. No matter your age, starting now is always worth it. Use this example to compare where you'll be in eight years if you do or don't get started today. By getting started today, you will earn more money over ten, twenty, thirty years than if you get started eight years from now.

You will always have plenty of reasons not to save. In your youth, it's easy to not think about retirement at all. Between the ages of twenty and sixty, expenses come from all directions: kids, houses, cars, colleges, taxes, healthcare. It might never feel like an ideal time to start saving. By that same logic, though, right now is the ideal time to start saving—because there will always be another expense.

Saving requires discipline. Pay yourself first by putting aside at least 10 percent of your income. After paying yourself, pay the rest of your bills. The sooner you implement this habit, the sooner you'll see your savings begin to grow. Otherwise, it'll become one of those great ideas that you never turn into reality. Start now. Don't just think about it. The sooner you start, the greater the effect of compound interest will be.

Step 2: Spend less than you earn.

Spending less than you earn may seem obvious, but often it goes ignored. Spending more than you've earned (after taxes) is a bad habit that afflicts people of all income levels. Those with less may feel that the extra expenses are a necessary evil, while those with more may assume their high income protects them from future financial trouble. This mindset prevents many people from building wealth.

I've known individuals who earn $40,000 per year but have the discipline to save $5,000 of it. Although it may seem like a small annual amount, that money, over time, adds up to future wealth and security. In contrast, I've met others who earn $1,000,000 per year and spend $1,100,000. This lack of discipline is a quick way to get into financial trouble, even if you have a high income.

People assume that if you drive a fancy car or live in an upscale neighborhood, you must be doing well financially. Research shows this assumption is only accurate about half the time. The rest of the time, people are living beyond their means. They have no savings, and their net worth is actually negative. They spend money faster than they earn it. They appear to be successful, but eventually they'll crash and be forced into reality.

Earning more money isn't a successful savings plan. The critical element of a successful savings plan is having the discipline to spend less than you earn, regardless of how much you make.

Step 3: Hire a competent financial adviser.

It has always been easier to lose money than it is to make and keep it. Most people who reach a certain wealth threshold recognize the importance of having an accountant and a lawyer. Many haven't discovered the benefits of a financial adviser. Based on the variety of investment options and the myriad people who call themselves financial advisers, it's easy to understand why. Figuring out who to work with can be so confusing that people give up and opt to manage their money themselves. Often, however, you may lose out on specialized expertise that a competent financial advisor can provide.

Bitcoin: It sounds like a flashy "go big or go home" opportunity, but it's not.

Bitcoin is a great example of how not to invest. One Christmas season, someone would corner me at every party I attended and quiz me about Bitcoin. Usually, they'd already invested and wanted me to validate their decision. Unfortunately, I didn't like what I'd seen of Bitcoin and couldn't recommend it.

Once an eighty-year-old client of mine trapped me in the hall at church and insisted I invest their account in Bitcoin. Despite their persistence, I gave my usual answer.

"No," I said. "It's not appropriate based on your risk tolerance or objectives." As they walked off upset, they snapped, "Well, then pray about it, and let me know—because I really feel like I should invest in it."

Like the Bitcoin craze, there have been too many market manias to count over the years. Manias have gone on as long as people have invested, including during the Dutch Tulip Mania of 1636, the 1720 South Sea Company crisis, and more recently, the 1999 dot-com bubble, the Enron scandal of 2001, and the 2008 mortgage crisis.

Human nature doesn't change.

A market commodity starts going up, and everyone piles on because they don't want to miss out. By definition, the masses get invested at the top of the bubble. Then it pops, and everyone laments how stupid it was to ultimately invest in nothing.

Bitcoin is extremely volatile and driven by so many market factors we don't understand that it is not a worthwhile "go big or go home" opportunity. Right now, the risk is just unnecessary when there are other, better risks you can take based on your personal risk tolerance.

For example, here's an important rule to know about Social Security: If you get married to someone before age sixty, you have to use your current spouse's work record or your own personal work record to claim Social Security. If you get married after age sixty, you can use any previous spouse's work records. I had a client named Betty who got remarried when she was fifty-nine *and a half*, following the death of her first husband. Since she didn't know about this Social Security rule, she had to use her current husband's work record on her Social Security claim.

Unfortunately, the work record of Betty's late husband was greater than either her own work record or her new husband's work record. This meant that because Betty was married six months before her sixtieth birthday, she had forfeited a $12,000 annual benefit. If she had known about the rule, Betty would have simply waited six months to get remarried. The only way she could use her late husband's work record to claim Social Security was to divorce her new spouse and then remarry him a few months down the road. So, what did Betty end up doing? Let's just say she made a call to her attorney after she spoke with me.

Managing your own investments can be done successfully, but it's not easy. First, it requires a time commitment to research and track your investments. Second, it requires discipline to stick with your strategy through challenging times. Third, and most difficult, it requires that you remove emotion from your investment process.

Finding the right adviser is more difficult than most people realize. Contrary to popular belief, the size of the advisor's firm or their brand popularity doesn't indicate the quality of the advice they provide. Part of the problem is that titles for financial sales representatives are unregulated. This means that brokers, annuity salesmen, and insurance agents can all call themselves financial advisers, financial consultants, financial planners, or whatever else they prefer. To avoid getting stuck with a salesperson when you're really looking for an adviser, make sure you ask these five questions:

1. Are you a fiduciary?

Unlike sales reps selling insurance, mutual funds, or other financial products, fiduciary advisors have a legal obligation to put your interests ahead of their own. Registered investment advisors and investment advisor representatives are fiduciaries. Only work with fiduciaries.

2. How many years have you been managing money for?

Longer is better. Choose an advisor who has lots of experience investing in both good and bad markets.

3. Can you show me your track record with previous clients' investments?

Showing you the record of a mutual fund, a hypothetical model, or anything else that they sell does not count. Any advisor who refuses to show you their actual track record should be crossed off your list. You must be able to see what they have actually done for their clients.

4. Are you paid by commission?

In the financial services industry, usually the worse the product is, the higher the commission is for its salesperson. The easiest way to avoid being sold a bad product is to avoid salespeople who receive commissions. I recommend you only work with advisors who are paid purely through advisory fees.

5. Does this product come with a surrender charge?

If a product has a surrender charge, it also has a commission. You should always be free to move your money out of an investment if you are dissatisfied. Don't choose a product that has a surrender charge.

Lastly, make sure you aren't paying too much for slow growth. Yes, it takes money to make money. But avoid these very expensive bad investments: annuities, insurance products, bank products, public real estate partnerships, oil and gas investments, and layered fees (like paying an advisor to invest in mutual funds).

Step 4: Avoid unnecessary debt.

Debt can be useful—if it's used properly.

When I went to Africa, I noticed that there were half-constructed buildings everywhere. When I asked my guide why, he told me they don't have a properly functioning banking system. Regular people have no way to borrow money, so they build what they can pay for now, then come back and build more next year when they have more money. In the meantime, half-finished buildings sit idle or get abandoned when the money never comes through.

If debt is used sparingly for assets that appreciate or allow you to make more money, taking out a loan makes sense. A house, a car, or potentially an education all make sense (up to a point).

Using debts for consumables or things that go down in value does not make sense. Impulse buying or buying on emotion are recipes for financial disaster. This is my definition of a credit card: a means of buying something unneeded, at a price you can't afford, with funds you don't have.

Most credit card debt pays for things that hurt rather than help your financial situation. Before you make any major purchase, decide whether it's a "need" or a "want." You'll be surprised how few purchases fall into the "need" category. Never go into debt for "wants."

Set a goal to live debt-free. Put a plan in place to reduce and then eliminate your debts. With a record 518.4 million credit cards in circulation in the United States (as of the beginning of 2023), an average household credit card balance of $7,486, and an average interest rate of 20 percent, it's no wonder so many households file for bankruptcy.[1]

Accumulating debt is the opposite of accumulating wealth. If you get stuck paying debts, you're hurting yourself and helping someone else accumulate wealth. With the few exceptions mentioned previously, avoid debt like the plague.

---

1 Daniel De Visé, "A Growing Number of Americans Face Potentially Crippling Credit-Card Debt," *The Hill,* January 21, 2023, https://thehill.com/business/3821799-a-growing-number-of-americans-face-potentially-crippling-credit-card-debt/, accessed October 2, 2023.

Step 5: Avoid large losses.

Money is slippery and difficult to keep. For each way we have to make money, ten ways exist to lose it. In my business, I'm constantly presented with investment opportunities. I may invest in one out of every twenty proposals that I review. Even with complete due diligence, some of those investments will be losers.

Investment losses are unavoidable. They come with the territory. The key is to minimize large losses that can quickly reverse the benefits of compound interest.

If you lose 25 percent of your portfolio, you need to make 33 percent to get back to even, which is workable. If you lose 50 percent of your portfolio, you have to make 100 percent to get back to even, a much more difficult task. A loss of 90 percent of your portfolio requires a gain of 900 percent to get back to even. Forget about it.

The key is to build a portfolio that is structured to avoid big, dramatic losses. Part of this step is avoiding financial decisions that ensure you never see the money you invest again. First, avoid scams; if it sounds too good to be true, it usually is. When you fall for a scam, that money you spend is just gone. You have very little recourse. Second, whenever possible, avoid giving loans to children, relatives, and friends. In my experience, these are not loans in most cases—because they're never paid back. Find other ways to help your family and friends.

Step 6: Follow a sound, long-term strategy.

Most investors don't follow a strategy: a disciplined, systematic process when making investment decisions. As a result, their investment portfolio often represents a patchwork of uncorrelated ideas that various salespeople have sold to them over many years.

Here are the three elements of a long-term strategy:

1. Properly select your risk tolerance.

Decide in advance how much risk or volatility you can subject your account to. For some investors, this means taking no risk at all and being willing to accept low returns in exchange for zero volatility. For others, it means trying to generate much higher returns while enduring the necessary roller-coaster ride to get there. Most investors end up somewhere in between these two extremes.

Identifying your risk tolerance is the single most important step to achieving long-term investment success. If it's set too low, you won't generate the returns you should. If it's set too high, should market conditions become difficult, you'll likely change strategies at the wrong time and suffer losses. This may kill your chances for outstanding long-term returns.

2. Follow a proven investment strategy that doesn't simply involve gut feelings.
Emotional investing is a recipe for failure. Investing is counterintuitive because doing what "feels good" often doesn't work. The market usually does the opposite of what most investors hope, think, or feel it should do. Once you begin to hope an investment will move in your favor, you're usually in trouble.

One of the models we use at Paragon tracks investor sentiment. It measures the percentage of investors that are optimistic and the percentage that are pessimistic at any point in time. When most investors are optimistic and think the market will go up, it goes down. Likewise, when most investors think the market will go down, it goes up. We measure this statistically, helping us increase or decrease our investment exposure.[2]

My recommendation is to choose an investment strategy that's driven by quantitative models that seek to proactively position your accounts for the most benefit in ever-changing market environments. Remove emotion from your strategy by including as many factors as possible from the list below:

- Your strategy works over different time frames.
- Your strategy provides effective rather than traditional diversification.
- Your strategy works in both bull and bear markets.
- Your strategy is disciplined, yet flexible and evolving.

---

2 See Appendix A for disclosures.

- Your strategy reduces risk and provides some level of downturn protection.

- Your strategy generates better returns than traditional stock indexes.

- Your strategy has a proven long-term track record.

3. Diversify your investments properly.

Without proper diversification, you will have no protection during a downturn. If all your investments behave the same, your portfolio isn't properly diversified. Essentially, make sure you don't put all your eggs in one basket. Most good investment advisors know to diversify through holding non-correlated assets that don't move up and down together in the same direction at the same time. At Paragon, rather than diversifying the traditional way by various asset classes, we believe it's more effective to diversify by various investment strategies.[3]

Step 7: Be patient.

We live in an "instant everything" world. Most of us have forgotten how to be patient. People, in general, want it all, and they want it now. They don't think in terms of paying the price or investing for the long-term. They act on a whim rather than follow a long-term plan.

Utah's Mountain View High School had a very successful track team, with several nationally ranked runners. I asked their coach at the time, James, why his runners were so successful. I thought he would tell me strategies that helped his athletes run faster. Instead, James explained that much of their success came from learning to pace themselves. They cultivated the patience to wait for the perfect time to make their final move to win the race.

When I big game hunt, I focus on finding animals that have "record book" potential. To locate them, I backpack into places rarely traveled. Oftentimes, I come back empty-handed. While several factors contribute to my success, extreme patience has been the most significant.

---

3 See Appendix A for disclosures.

Patience is also a key attribute for successful investors. As soon as you put a solid strategy in place, it's all about patience, self-control, discipline, and, of course, more patience.

This is one of the most difficult steps for investors. A lack of patience has ruined many sound investment plans. We position our funds to take advantage of the market, but we never truly know when we're going to be rewarded. Sometimes we spend months or years waiting. Following this process, though, can yield tremendous rewards.

The market does its best to make investors give up at the worst possible time. At Paragon, our best returns almost always follow the years we have lackluster performance. Unfortunately, the investors who didn't exercise patience and stay invested during the rough times missed out on those returns. Patience keeps you focused on the big picture and is critical to long-term investment success.

Risk Tolerance, Increasing Your Odds, and Keeping Your Options Open

The seven steps I discussed are designed to help you build wealth, regardless of how much money you have today.[4] You will have noticed several overlaps between these steps and how I hunted leopard in Africa, like needing mental toughness, commitment, patience, and a trustworthy guide. You'll see these themes deepen in other hunting stories throughout this book.

Whether you're building financial or true wealth (that broader and more authentic experience of deep happiness, fulfillment, and success), these steps are vital to making good on the principle of "go big or go home." By putting them into action, you'll see your skill, confidence, and thirst to pass up safe opportunities grow. The path to building wealth takes time. It requires good strategy and the patience to stay invested through the ups and downs.

What will the result be?

Extraordinary opportunities and outcomes.

---

4 See Appendix A for disclosures.

I've been interviewed by a variety of media about a range of topics, from my entrepreneurialism to my leadership at Paragon and, of course, my more recent foray into municipal governance. One time, a magazine journalist asked me, "Did you think you might fail? What was your Plan B and Plan C?"

I answered, "I never thought I would fail."

Failure is not an option in the "go big or go home" approach to life. Mistakes and hardships are not failures. They are opportunities to learn and grow. That means you don't have to be perfect or make the right decision every single time to successfully incorporate this principle into your life. You don't have to be fearless or even a thrill-seeker either. What you have to do is act according to your own risk tolerance. (See step six.)

Envision what you want, push your limits, make a solid plan, and follow through. Through this, you'll be able to increase your risk incrementally over time as you gain experience and confidence. At any given moment, what one person thinks is a huge risk may look like small potatoes to another person. That does not matter one bit, and that's why the "go big or go home" principle is equally attainable for everyone.

Commit to your own vision and goals based on *your* risk tolerance. Then do whatever you have to do to achieve those goals. If you set your risk tolerance correctly, that will allow you to stay invested through the difficult times and will increase the likelihood that you will achieve what you've envisioned. This is why it's so critical to identify your level of risk tolerance correctly.

It's important to remember that when everything is on the line, most people are less likely to take big risks. In investing, I recommend my clients not take huge risks unless their portfolios are sufficiently diverse. This is how I would respond if you came to me as a new client and said you want to invest a million dollars:

"Great. We need to structure this so that you're going to be okay as we go through the market's ups and downs. The last thing you should do is bail out along the way. If you bail out, you'll bail out at the wrong time—because most people bail out when the markets are down. And that's always a mistake."

If you begin by taking more risk than you can handle, then you're going to want to bail, and you'll never achieve the wealth you're looking for. To mitigate that reaction, I ratchet down the risk to a level that I think you're comfortable with. In this investing scenario, acceptable risk is defined as not caring about the downs because you're confident the ups will get you where you want to go. You've got your money invested; you're watching the market do its thing; the Dow drops 1,000 points; and you don't care because you're structured in such a way that you trust it will work out in the long run.

You trust me to guide you there, just as I trust my guides and their experience when I go extreme hunting. I do my research and due diligence to make sure I choose the right guide. And I accept that I need to hire a professional because I know I shouldn't go on extreme big game hunts alone. Having a guide increases my odds for success.

Life success is about increasing your odds and having options.

You never want to box yourself into a situation where you don't have options. As soon as you do that, as soon as you only have one option, all you can do is hope it works out. You've got to be in a position where you always have options. That's how you live the "go big or go home" principle, no matter your risk tolerance.

You'll see the theme of risk recur in the hunting stories and lessons throughout this book. Wealth never comes without risk, and when all is said and done, risk is what makes life an adventure. Don't forget that there's freedom in adventure, and adventure doesn't have to mean flying by the seat of your pants or taking up an extreme sport. You need a plan. In the next chapter, a story about hunting grizzly bears in Alaska, I jump right into discussing the importance of doing your research and due diligence in more detail.

CHAPTER 3

HUNTING GRIZZLY BEAR IN ALASKA

R esearch is a big part of making a hunt successful.

Step one is to figure out where big animals with good genetics live. Even if a species is found all over the place, they won't all have the same quality of genetics that big game hunters look for. To do my research, I read magazines and search trophy record books to see where those animals have been killed. If I can't find the information I need in books, I'll call up the hunters who have already killed trophy animals. I'll talk to them about where they went, what type of experience they had, and what guides they used. I also reach out to taxidermists and ask them about their biggest animals and where they came from. I speak with game biologists and outfitters too.

The real challenge is figuring out who's full of crap and who's not. I always vet them and do my due diligence. It's not that difficult to call yourself an outfitter and charge someone a bunch of money to take them hunting. If they're unsuccessful, then they say, "That's why it's called hunting." But that reasoning is pretty lame. Trips are never guaranteed. Hunters can spend huge amounts of money and effort to get somewhere they should never have gone to in the first place.

And because I go after big animals, I need the best guides and gear. I have to know that I'm looking in the right place for the right animal. I also have to know that I can hit my target and have enough firepower so that when those ten seconds arrive and I pull the trigger, that animal is going to die. The serious trophy hunting I do requires a whole different level of both preparation and execution.

Why You Need to Invest in the Best Hunting Gear

Over 1,000 nights camping in the backcountry have made me very picky about my hunting gear. I've always tried to buy the best gear available, even when I didn't have that much money. Rather than writing a check every other year and having a closet full of mediocre junk, I prefer to write a check *once* for quality equipment.

If I have to choose between buying a nice bow for $800 or a phenomenal bow for $1,600, I'll always go for the more expensive option—if I'm fairly certain I'll enjoy it more and it's going to last longer. In the long run, it actually costs less. The quality of the gear I use reflects this buying philosophy. It's how I could pass along a pair of forty-five-year-old binoculars to my son Austin. They still work great today because they were such high quality when I bought them.

Being prepared isn't just a Boy Scout motto. In extreme conditions, it's the difference between life and death. On top of being a sound use of my money, I've always bought the best quality gear available because it provides me the protection I need to go anywhere at any time of the year.

If you get into trouble in the middle of nowhere, no one is coming to your rescue. You can't dial 9-1-1. You can't run to the store or place an online order for delivery. Let me tell you, if you find yourself stranded on top of a mountain, convinced you're not going to make it down before you freeze to death, the amount of money you're willing to spend on winter gear will increase dramatically. That's why extreme hunters say their backpack is their lifeline.

When you hike and climb for days in remote mountains, across deserts, or through gnarly forests, your backpack holds the gear that will save your hide when you get stuck or injured. It holds your food, water, hunting gear, and everything else you need to stay alive in all conditions. A serious hunter's backpack rarely weighs less than forty-five pounds, but you never leave it behind.

Mother Nature is beautiful and spectacular, but she's also very unforgiving. In an emergency situation, you may not get a second chance. I always include a satellite transponder, enough water and food to get me back to civilization, and proper clothing to stay protected from freezing weather or unexpected downpours. Quality sleeping gear is also a must.

Besides making sure I've got the right gear to keep me alive, it takes time to travel to the location I'm hunting, figure out the terrain, locate a trophy animal, and put together a strategy to gain an advantage over it. On average, I spend nine days in the field—much longer than most hunters. But hunting the type of trophies I'm interested in requires extreme time commitments. Then, after all that work, it usually comes down to only five or ten minutes for me to get in position, verify the wind speed, distance, and angle to target, stabilize my weapon with a dead rest, get the animal in my crosshairs, focus on my breathing, and slowly pull the trigger or release my arrow.

My point is that the success of an entire hunt comes down to only a few minutes. (That's true whether a hunter spends one day, three days, or nine days in the field.) And during those minutes, I'm under pressure to execute perfectly. I sure wouldn't want to miss the opportunity I made possible through all my preparation and hard work just because a piece of my gear—rifle, bullets, bow, arrows, binoculars, spotting scope—doesn't work properly. Would you? *(continues on next page)*

So, to recap: why should you invest in quality hunting gear? It makes better financial sense. It will save your life. And it'll increase the odds you get the animal you've put so much time and energy into hunting.

Here's a list of some of the gear I use:

- Camouflage clothing: base layer, mid layer, outer layers—Sitka and Kuiu
- Hats, gloves, socks: Sitka and Kuiu; Darn Tough Vermont for socks
- Boots: Kenetrek and Zamberlan
- Backpacks: Stone Glacier, Mystery Ranch, Sitka, Kuiu, Badlands
- Rifles: McWhorter Custom 300 Ultra Mag, Gunwerks 6.5 PRC
- Muzzleloader: McWhorter Custom 45 Caliber
- Bows: Hoyt, Mathews, and PSE
- Knives: Benchmade, Böker, and high-end Browning
- Binoculars: Zeiss Victory RF 10x42, Swarovski Optik 10x56
- Spotting scopes: Swarovski STX 25x60 with accessories
- Best quality optics for the price: Vortex binoculars and scopes
- GPS and satellite communication: Garmin and Zoleo
- Tents: Hilleberg and Big Agnes
- Sleeping bags and pads: Western Mountaineering, Mountain Hardware, Therm-a-rest
- Cooking: Jetboil, MSR WhisperLite
- Water filters: Sawyer, Katadyn, MSR Guardian
- Mapping apps and software: OnX Hunt, BaseMap
- Hunting info services: Huntin' Fool, goHunt, Muley Crazy, Gear Junkie, Backpacker

Early in my career, I shot a huge elk in New Mexico with a 7mm Remington Magnum from about 450 yards across a canyon. By the time I crossed the canyon to reach it, the elk had gotten up and disappeared into the dark. (You never chase an animal in the dark.) The next day, I returned to the blood trail. It had snowed eighteen inches overnight, making it impossible to track. I could tell the elk had been bleeding out, but we never found it again. That shouldn't have happened. It suffered because of my firepower error. After that experience, I went home and did my research to learn more about the best ballistics and calibres I needed. That led me to switch from a 7mm mag to a 300 ultra mag rifle.

In May 1996, I went to Alaska to hunt for a trophy grizzly bear. This would be a coastal grizzly, also known as a brown bear, which are bigger than interior grizzlies that live inland.

I'd met a hunting guide named Dale Adams, in his forties with a beard, built like me and obsessed with hunting. For his regular job, he owned and ran a sixty-foot commercial fishing boat. Dale reminded me of Al Gilliam, also a very serious, hard-core guide. Dale lamented that no one ever kills *big* bears. They killed bears all right, but typically average sized. He wanted to kill a *big* bear.

"Dale," I told him. "I'm your guy—and I'll come and stay as long as I need to. Let's get a big bear."

Shawn came with me on this trip. At eleven years old, he'd almost finished fifth grade. Kids that young don't usually come on hunts this deep into the backcountry. As a rule of thumb, they should be avoiding grizzly bears. But Shawn had nerves of steel and a thirst for adventure, so I decided to bring him along.

We flew from Salt Lake City to Seattle, then on to Ketchikan, Alaska. During a four-hour layover, we walked two miles to an outdoor shopping area in downtown Ketchikan, where we ate chili dogs and bought waders for Shawn. Shawn didn't want waders because he thought they would slow him down in the event that he had to run away from a bear.

"Wear them anyway," I told him, chuckling. "You'll thank me when you don't freeze solid."

From Ketchikan, we flew to Sitka, Alaska, where we met Dale and our second guide and cook, Frank, at the airport. Another hunter named Joe, who was being guided by Frank, also came with us. We stayed at a local hotel that looked like a log cabin and walked around Sitka, a truly beautiful place. After a great dinner cooked by Frank, a professional chef, we turned in for the night.

Dale picked us up at 7:00 a.m. so that we could get our bear permits from the Department of Fish and Game. Then we headed to the Celtic Air, his commercial fishing boat. Dale fished salmon. The leading cause of death on this very old-school boat happens when a crew member goes up on deck at night to take a leak over the side and falls overboard in the rough water. The rest of the crew don't even realize he's gone until morning.

We left Sitka and traveled to the head of Slocum Arm, arriving by five o'clock in the afternoon. That evening, Frank cooked us another great meal, a big spaghetti dinner. While Shawn and Joe stayed on the boat after our meal, Frank, Dale, and I loaded up in a skiff, a small aluminum boat with a 15-horsepower motor on the back. We made our way to the shore to see if we could find any bears. Flying over big, choppy waves, the goal of that ride was to not get swamped on the way.

This coastal part of Alaska is gorgeous. It's full of saltwater inlets, windswept beaches, and pine forests. We spent three hours glassing various beaches, meaning we used our binoculars and spotting scopes to look for animals at a distance. We spotted a sow and her two cubs. Bears and pigs share the same vernacular: females are called sows, and males are called boars.

Jumping back into the skiff, we moved closer to get a better look. In a back cut of the forest, we saw what appeared to be a large, dark-colored bear. Boars are usually a darker chocolate brown, whereas sows are a lighter medium brown with a bit of blond mixed in. Males also tend to have bigger, boxier bodies.

We beached the skiff and began to stalk the bear. Coming over a knoll, we found it feeding about 100 yards away. Unfortunately, the direction of the wind betrayed us, carrying our scent to the bear. Bears can't see that well, but they have an incredible sense of smell.

The bear whirled and took off into the brush.

We got back in the skiff and decided to leave the area so that it could calm down. Over the next couple hours, we glassed more beaches and saw several black-tailed deer, two small fawns, and a dozen eagles circling what must have been a bear carcass.

Sows and their cubs prefer to stay in one area, while boars often wander afield until they find a sow in heat. If the boar happens upon a sow with cubs, he will kill the cubs so that the sow goes back into heat. Not surprisingly, then, sows and cubs run from boars. A big boar can kill up to fourteen cubs a year. So, when anyone gives me crap about killing a single boar, I tell them those stats. I'm effectively saving dozens of baby bears. Thank you very much. On top of that, at certain times of the year, hunters in Alaska aren't legally required to keep the meat from a bear. So a big bear that's killed can also feed a range of wildlife in the area, including eagles and wolves.

Before returning to the Celtic Air for the night, we did return to the last place where we'd seen the big boar. We waited until dark but didn't catch another glimpse of it.

The following day, Shawn, Dale, and I traveled to Klag Bay and went by skiff to a mountain peak called The Sisters. To get there, we had to go through a nasty channel of whirlpools.

In this part of Alaska, the ocean and inland lakes are connected by short, narrow rivers called inlets. Whirlpools are caused by the clash of salt water being pushed inland by the tide during the day and the fresh water from lakes being sucked out as the tide changes.

Whirlpools appeared and disappeared all around our skiff. Some of them could span twenty feet across and the eyes at their centers up to five feet deep. Weaving across the water, we did our level best to avoid them. But on our way out of the inlets after dark, avoiding them became almost impossible.

"Watch out!" Dale shouted. All of a sudden, a whirlpool opened beneath us, and the boat dropped five feet straight down. As soon as we felt that drop, Dale gunned the motor to put on a burst of speed that got us out of the whirlpool in the nick of time. Otherwise the boat would have been sucked into it, and we'd have been gone.

It was pretty crazy, and the danger very real. White crosses lined a stretch of the bank where whirlpools had sucked in more than one traveler. That week, in fact, four hunters drowned in the same area as us. We learned about the tragedy when the Coast Guard came across our radio as they tried to find the hunters. A bigger issue than the whirlpools themselves was the cold water, which will quickly put you into hypothermia. Life jackets just make it more likely the bodies will be found.

Late that afternoon, we took the skiff around a corner and spotted a boar feeding in the forest line. The wind still wasn't cooperating with us, so we shut off the motor to see if we could sneak up on the bear by drifting and rowing.

Shawn acted as lookout while Dale and I rowed. "Row," he'd whisper whenever the bear lowered its head to feed. Then, "Stop," when the bear lifted his head. "Row. Stop. Row. Stop. Row. Stop."

For forty-five minutes, we drew closer and closer to the bear without it noticing. It's all about patience. The bear looked really good, like it might be a shooter. Finally, we got to shore and snuck across the beach. Within sixty yards of it, we paused and looked the bear over.

We decided not to shoot. The bear was a good size, but not the monster we'd thought he might be. That's the way it is when hunting for a big bear. Often you'll find yourself passing up a number of decent-sized bears that most hunters would shoot in a heartbeat.

Back on the Celtic Air, we had a turkey dinner and ice cream for dessert. Shawn did some fishing and caught a 25-pound halibut, which excited him to no end.

The next day, the Celtic Air took us to Fordham, another remote island thirteen hours away. At half past four o'clock in the afternoon, we went out and glassed for hours. Before nightfall, we came across a sprawling, beautiful flat that edged a swath of pine forest. The grass reached three feet tall, so we hid in it and got comfortable, sitting until dark.

We did catch a glimpse of several bear legs walking in the bush, but never got a good look at most of them. The one bear we did see clearly turned out to be a big, blocky sow. That sized sow could trick another hunter into thinking she was a boar; luckily, the two cubs with her tipped us off.

While Joe, Dale, and I went hunting, Shawn and Frank stayed back and caught a bunch of fish in the afternoon, so we ate very well. A veritable fish feast.

The next day, we went by skiff on a long trip all the way back to the head of Slocum. We glassed a lot of country, but only saw two bears. They moved so fast, we only had eyes on them for a few seconds before they disappeared into the timber. Bears run a lot faster than humans. The pair had looked to be a sow and a boar, so we waited to see if they'd come back out. They never did.

Around dark, we beached the skiff and hiked into a big meadow. A sow and her two cubs hung out at the back of the cut, and for once the wind had turned in the right direction. We snuck within fifty yards of them. Eventually, they spooked and took off into the woods.

Calling an end for the day, we returned to the Celtic Air to claim our consolation prize: another big feast.

To switch things up a bit the next day, we visited an abandoned gold shaft in the morning. The gold rush had been very big up in this part of the world. Shawn and I had a blast looking around. Dale had been teasing Shawn about gnomes, swearing up and down that they were real, so we made an inside joke of it at this mine and set out to "find" one. In Alaska, they're a people version of what we call "snipes." Some people swear gnomes are real. We did find a hat that had been dropped at some point; of course, we all decided it must have belonged to a gnome. Shawn was exhilarated.

That evening, we boated all over Slocum. Wildlife roamed everywhere: sows, cubs, a few eagles, sea otters, geese, one lone small bear. No big bears, though.

Other than the possible big bear that we'd seen on the first day, within the first hour, we hadn't seen a giant. We were starting to feel the pressure. Would we ever see the Mr. Big that we'd come to Alaska to get?

When Joe and Dale saw a big bear with a bad left leg on the same meadow where we'd seen the sow and cubs two nights ago, they nicknamed him Tripod because he only had three good legs. Joe took a shot from about 140 yards away, but he missed. The bear got away. Joe was not a happy camper that night. Usually on these hunts, you only get one chance at a good bear.

Before we set out in the skiff the following morning, Frank, our guide, told me, "My gun's got issues. Don't count on me for backup. I'll need to get this fixed."

We went back to The Sisters in the skiff. The weather had turned bad, which made the ride out on the water miserable. In the rain and wind, with huge waves and whitecaps, the small, fourteen-foot skiff started to feel very insignificant. Glassing through the binoculars became almost impossible.

Frank and I managed to eyeball a black spot that looked out of place about 100 yards from the bank. In that weather, we couldn't tell if it was a bear. After several minutes, the black spot started moving quickly toward the tree line.

"Oh, shiz!" I said. "That's a huge grizzly bear."

It reached the edge of the grassy knoll between the bank and forest, stood up on its hind legs, then whirled and took off into the trees. We went ashore and set up about a hundred yards from where the bear had gone into the woods. A little while later, a bear came out of the woods about a mile away from us.

"We better go check that out," Frank said, since Mr. Big likely wouldn't come back out tonight. Usually, when a bear spooks the way that big one had, you won't see it again for a few days, if at all.

We hiked back to the skiff, hopped in, and moved down the beach to glass the new bear. It wasn't a shooter, so we headed back and hoped Mr. Big would come back out at nightfall, which would come in about two and a half hours.

That afternoon, the three of us—Frank, Shawn, and I—headed back to where we'd last seen the big bear. Frank and Shawn set up next to a rock formation right at the tree line while I went out into the grassy knoll to glass for bears on the other side of the rock. Suddenly, a stone landed at my feet, and I turned to see Frank and Shawn looking very concerned and pointing to the right. They'd thrown it. My gaze snapped past them; fifty yards from them, a huge bear came out of the trees.

The bear couldn't see them yet, but it might have been able to smell them. And it could definitely see me. Effectively pinned to the rock, Frank and Shawn had nowhere to go. Their eyes were as big as saucers.

I dropped down and crawled through the tall grass toward my gun about twenty yards away. I hadn't forgotten that I couldn't rely on Frank for backup because his gun had been acting up. That put more pressure on me.

Thankfully, I reached my gun. The bear hadn't seen Frank and Shawn yet, but it sensed our presence and moved forward, trying to figure out what was going on.

"Shoot," Frank called. "He's huge. Shoot!"

In the tall grass, I couldn't set up a dead rest. Quickly, I pushed myself into a kneeling position and sighted on the bear about twenty yards away. The animal was so large and close that I had to aim upward. My adrenaline spiked. I shot.

Boom, boom, boom. Three shots in five seconds.

All three shots were direct hits. The first shot struck behind the bear's left shoulder, and the force spun it around. The second shot hit behind its right shoulder. The bear stood up and kept coming straight toward me. My third shot hit it at the base of the neck.

The bear went down. After thirteen days, we had our only chance, and we got him. Finally!

When you're hunting dangerous predators like this, you experience day after day of boredom, followed by one exhilarating moment of intense terror, then the thrill of the shot, then relief like I was feeling at this very moment. After that, it's celebration. But before the celebrating, you've essentially had to go from zero to a hundred miles an hour instantly, then bam—you shoot, the animal dies, you take seconds to make sure it's dead, and then you come down off that surge of adrenaline going from sheer terror to success.

Once the initial excitement over killing this enormous bear died down, we got organized. Frank called on the radio for Dale and Joe to bring their skiff over and help us pack the bear and all our gear up.

We set to work caping the bear. The danger doesn't end after you've killed an animal. The process of removing its hide and preparing the parts that need to be transported require a degree of caution. Out in the wild, someone always has to keep watch in case another predator comes along wanting that carcass for itself.

In 2021, a hunter in Alaska killed a moose twenty miles from where I'd been hunting at the time. While the hunter caped that moose, a grizzly bear caught him unaware, attacked, and killed him. Wolves can also be a significant danger in many places, especially when they travel in packs.

"Wow!" Frank said suddenly. He held something up. "Here's your bullet."

Very rarely does a hunter get to keep his killing bullet, in this case from a .338 Magnum. But this bear was so large and gnarly that its hide had stopped the bullet from exiting its body. The bullet had entered behind its shoulder and traveled through the lung up to the middle of the back.

Frank kept caping the back of the bear. "No freakin' way," he exclaimed, and held up my second bullet. It had come to a stop next to the first bullet, entering behind the bear's other shoulder and traveling to meet it at the top of the back. Now that was perfection.

I still have those two bullets.

The hide measured out to a conservative nine feet, four inches. Stretched out, I could have made a case for nine feet, eight inches, but I went with the average: nine feet, six inches. The width from left front paw to right front paw measured ten feet, six inches. This was officially a ten-foot square bear.

Grizzly bears are much larger than black bears, and interior grizzly bears are smaller than the grizzlies on the coast. The largest are Kodiak bears, a subspecies native to Kodiak Island off the Alaska coast. In general, the farther north you go up the coast, the bigger the grizzly bears get. That meant we had been hunting at a disadvantage by staying in the southeast—which only made this trophy sweeter.

"This is the largest bear I've ever taken," said Dale, excited. "It'll also be the second largest bear ever taken in Southeast Alaska. And the largest taken in the last thirty years."

The Department of Fish and Game in Sitka confirmed it. The bear taken thirty years prior had been controversial; several people claimed it had been taken farther north because it was just so much larger than the other bears registered in the southeast, but the Department of Fish and Game had accepted it into the record book.

Joe and Dale went back to The Sisters, across from where we'd gotten our grizzly. They shot another bear, smaller but decent sized. That bear let out an unbelievable roar before charging them from about twenty-five yards away. They fired nine shots to put it down, which is definitely more common than just three shots. To kill a bear, you have to hit its heart or lungs. That's tough to do when they're such large animals. Hitting it anywhere else just pisses a big bear off.

Dale ended up delivering the two kill shots at close range with his .458 Winchester Magnum. It was a close call.

After they caped the bear out, we took the Celtic Air to another black bear hunting area nineteen hours away. Out there in the middle of nowhere, we came across a huge 300-foot waterfall. What a spectacular sight. Reading it on a map completely missed the enormity of it. In the rest of the United States, that waterfall would have been designated a national park. But up in Alaska, it's just one more majestic sight that almost no one ever sees. That level of the beauty and wildness of the country will stay with me forever.

When we got back in the skiff for another day of hunting, we set out to find a black bear this time. We got within twelve feet of one. Shawn started breathing heavily, rattled for once, and we ended up letting it go. We saw a second bear that had a rubbed hide, and we played cat and mouse with a third bear in a dense tree line. We couldn't quite get a good enough look at him, so we moved on.

We had a great time hunting in black bear country, but never found any giants. As the trip came to a close, Dale and Frank took the boat back. Then a four-person seaplane came to pick Shawn, Joe, and me up. Fog made it very tricky; if it's too thick, the plane can't land or take off. We had to wait for a break in the cover. The plane didn't have instrumentation, so the pilot navigated only by visual. We finally got a temporary break in the fog and took off. As the plane gained altitude, we watched the fog close beneath us. It was quite a sight, and dangerous; we literally flew fifty yards above the granite peaks below us. Back then, that type of small plane went down often throughout Alaska. Before getting in it, we had to sign a waiver relieving the pilot and company of all liability.

The level of risk that you're willing to take really depends on the return that you're hunting. As you get more and more aggressive about that return, if you take more risk than you should, the consequences can be devastating. Success in life and the investment markets require you to take calculated risks. It's critical that you are fully aware and understand the risks you're taking. If you don't get that piece of the puzzle right, the possibility of failure increases significantly. But each person has to make a judgment call for themselves. On this hunt, we made it home safely, and the reward for our risk was a monster grizzly bear.

CHAPTER 4

BUILD SOLID RELATIONSHIPS; VALUE YOUR FRIENDS, FAMILY, AND COMMUNITY

I f you break down everything you might have in your life, relationships are the most important—not your house, your car, or your boat. Relationships are the essence of life. They're the foundation of achieving true wealth, and the quality of your relationships will determine the quality of your life. That's why building solid personal and professional relationships matters. Showing your family, friends, and community how much you love, value, and are grateful for them matters too.

Value Your Family

My family is my greatest treasure. I value them above all else, beginning with my wife Cathy. We were married in the Salt Lake City Temple in 1979. That means we've been together nearly forty-five years—and counting! She's my best friend and my partner. Cathy loves her kids, her grandkids, and a clean house. She'll also tell you that more than a decade before I became mayor, *she* was the one actively involved in politics. Cathy loves it when her political candidates win.

Cathy herself is a leader. She has served as the Relief Society President in our ward at church and is always helping other people—visiting them in their homes, finding out what they need. She's also super generous, almost to a fault. For thirteen years she decorated cool Christmas trees and donated them to the Festival of Trees for auction, with proceeds going to the Primary Children's Hospital. My wife loves Christmas so much, she tells us, "When I'm dead, I want Christmas tree lights hung on my casket." Before Cathy stopped decorating trees to focus on the Live Your Dream Foundation, her trees, with their colorful oversized ornaments, auctioned for $4,000 to $5,000, all for charity.

Cathy will tell you that she hasn't lived a boring life. I could share dozens of stories about our adventurous life, but I'll share just a couple of stories for fun.

Early in my career when I performed as a magician, I once put Cathy (involuntarily) in a magic sword box made for a 110-pound assistant. That was a show in front of 800 people. At the time, Cathy was eight and a half months pregnant. She didn't appreciate me doing that, but she was a good sport and went along with it.

Another time I called Cathy after getting that trophy grizzly bear that I just told you about in Chapter 3. I was in the middle of nowhere in Alaska on a sixty-foot fishing boat with no cell phone coverage. It was about the thirteenth day of the trip, and it'd been really difficult to get any call through to my wife.

When I finally got on a marine radio so I could make the call, we had to align the ridges and point the radio toward a crevasse through the mountains just to get service. After that, I had to go through at least four operators to reach her! It was a frickin' project just to call my wife!

Twenty minutes later, I got Cathy on the phone.

"Hello," she said, not knowing it was me.

"Hey, this is Dave! How's it goin'?"

"Oh my gosh," she said. "I've been wondering how you are. Are you okay?"

"Yeah, I'm fine."

"Did you get the bear?" she asked.

We had talked before about how I was going to try and find a *monster* bear.

"Yeah, I got the bear."

Without missing a beat, Cathy said, "It's not coming in our house."

Now, when you realize that's the first time we'd talked in thirteen days, and within the first thirty seconds of our conversation, she declared, "It's not coming in our house," you know Cathy can hold her own. This would be a BIG bear, and she didn't want any battle over where that gigantic, mounted animal would be going. Cathy always tells it like it is. I never have to wonder what she thinks.

The ten-foot-square grizzly bear is now located on a wooden stand in the southeast corner of Paragon's conference room. He's looking toward the conference room table growling, with his left front paw balancing on a rock and the right paw hovering off the ground, ready to take a swipe at anything that gets in his way.

True Love and Marriage

My marriage to Cathy works because we're both very independent. Cathy's not needy at all. Her girlfriends sometimes ask her what she thinks about me going off hunting for so long, which isn't cheap. "Are you okay with that?" they ask. "Do you like to go on hunts?"

"No," she'll say, "the only kind of hunting I like is in a mall." Then she'll pull out her Visa and say, "I'm deadly with this."

From my relationship with Cathy, I know marriage can bring couples more joy and happiness than anything in life. It can be amazing! It can also be difficult. No marriage, no partnership is easy. As human beings, we're always focused on our own self-interest. That's normal. But for us to succeed—really succeed—in marriage, we have to be willing to put our partner's best interests in front of our own. True love is caring more about your partner than you care about yourself.

Although I'm not a preacher in the traditional sense, I do have the authority to marry people in Utah. So in 2019, when my son Austin and his fiancé Brooke asked me to perform their marriage, I shared three recommendations with them for a long, happy, and successful marriage. These recommendations apply to living a happy life, too, which I consider much more valuable than money.

Do Not Judge. Jesus Christ said, "Thou shalt not judge, for with that same judgement ye judge, ye shall also be judged" (Matt 7:1–2). That message alone should be incentive enough not to judge others. It seems simple, but it requires effort to not pass judgment on others. Likewise, it requires effort to not pass judgment on your spouse. Judging in a relationship sets up one person as superior and the other as subordinate. In marriage, you must be equal partners, working together to live a happy and fulfilling life. Judging each other flies in the face of putting each other first. Do not judge your spouse or others.

Show Unconditional Love. Unconditional love is just that—love that has no conditions. It's loving someone for who they are, not loving them because they do what you want. You understand they make mistakes. You can't control their behavior, but you can control whether you love them or not. Because everyone is self-interest driven, showing unconditional love can be difficult to implement in real life. However, showing that kind of love is the solution to the most difficult of interpersonal relationships. That's why Jesus Christ taught us not just to love, but to love unconditionally.

Just Be Nice. Another simple principle, but under the stresses of life, just being nice can be more difficult than it seems. What's easy is being impatient, unkind, or quick to anger, which usually sets off a chain of negative events. One negative thing leads to another until the situation becomes much worse than it needs to be. The solution? Just be nice!

Regardless of how stressed you get, regardless of what's going wrong in your life, regardless of whether you're tired or hungry, regardless of whether you feel misunderstood or mistreated: Just be nice. When you feel the stress rising and think you're being treated unfairly, think to yourself, "Just be nice."

People spend so much time accomplishing their to-do list: cooking, working, cleaning, taking care of themselves, running around, being ultra-busy. The benefit of all that activity pales in comparison to the benefit of practicing, "Just be nice." Don't ever raise your voice to each other. Just be nice.

Over the course of your life, I honestly believe that whether you're "nice" or not has a lot to do with how you'll be remembered. Being nice, especially to your spouse, is one of the most important things you can do to live a happy life of true wealth.

No Family Is Perfect

One thing to know about my marriage, my kids, and my family, in general, is that we're not perfect. No family is. We've faced our share of troubles. In this chapter, I'm telling you a bit about our real lives to give you a glimpse into the good, the bad, and sometimes the ugly that *all* families deal with, regardless of how much money they have or not. Also, you should know that when it comes to sharing about some of my family's challenges, I've run all this by my wife and kids to get their okay about any of the details I've included here.

About ten years ago, a couple in their midfifties came into my office to talk about their financial life—their investments, their estate plan, normal things I discuss with clients. It was the first time I'd met them, so we sat down and started having a good conversation. The husband was engaged; the wife was engaged. But I noticed the wife kept looking over at the picture of my family hanging on the wall. It's one of several family portraits Cathy and I have had taken over the years.

This portrait from 2010 included all five kids, three spouses, and our two grandkids at the time. The photographer had carefully arranged the twelve of us to be standing, kneeling, and sitting next to each other. We're all smiling and enjoying a gorgeous fall day up Provo Canyon. Bright orange and yellow aspen trees in their autumn glory stand out against the green pine forest. It was the perfect outdoor setting for capturing one ideal moment in our lives.

So that's the picture this wife kept looking at. Then, seemingly out of nowhere and off topic, she started breaking down and crying. "Everybody has a perfect family," she sobbed. "Our family has *all* these issues. I can't believe all the issues and challenges we face. This isn't how I envisioned raising a family when I was younger and growing up!"

She was really upset. Apparently, seeing my "perfect family" made her feel really bad. I had to step out of the office to get her some tissues.

When I came back, I told her, "You know, things aren't always the way they appear. We've had a lot of challenges in our family too. Everyone's going through things like this," I said.

Then I gave her a pep talk and assured her, "There *is* a path forward."

Over the years, my experience with this woman has stuck with me. As I share about being a husband, father, and grandfather, I want you to know how proud I am of my family and how much I want them to live happy, fulfilling lives of true wealth. I also want you to know that we've had to forge our own paths forward through good times and bad, including as we've dealt with life-changing issues like illness, addiction, divorce, and death.

Our Five Children

It's hard to believe, but our five kids now range from ages twenty-nine to forty-three. The first two, Shannon and Katie, came two years apart in 1980 and 1982. Then our next two children, Shawn and Kelli, came three and four years later in 1985 and 1989. Our last child, Austin, came five years later in 1994. We were losing enthusiasm as time went on!

My family has always had a ton of stuff going on, so I make it a priority to spend quality time with each of them. Over the last thirty years, we've loved making memories on family vacations at Lake Powell. I look forward to the peace of its clear blue water and gorgeous red rock canyons. Besides relaxing, we've loved waterskiing off our twenty-three-foot Cobalt ski boat. I've always been super careful about the kids' safety around water. With my youngest son Austin, I literally tied him to me when we slept at night on our houseboat. We now have to keep track of eleven grandkids, so everyone gets a life jacket with a buzzer that activates if it lands in the water.

When my five children graduated from high school, I personally took them each on three- and four-week senior trips somewhere in the world. Shannon and I traveled around Australia, Fiji, and New Zealand—a trip that opened her eyes to the world and got her excited to travel. Katie and I rented a piece of junk of a car that we drove 1,600 miles through Germany, Austria, Switzerland, and Italy. We were not allowed to rent a nice car because the rental company was concerned it might get stolen in Italy. I already told you about my harrowing hunting trip with Shawn to Zimbabwe and Botswana, Africa, in Chapter 1—quite a senior trip! Then Kelli and I traveled through Amsterdam, Tanzania, and back through Paris. The final senior trip I took was with Austin through London, Tanzania, Kenya, and back to Rome. On this trip, Austin told me he realized, "Life isn't about what you have; it's about who you have in your life and how you choose to spend your time. Experiences and the people you experience them with are all that really matter. Money and things don't matter nearly as much." I'm happy knowing Austin learned lessons like these that we've always tried to teach our kids.

Senior trips with my five children made for unforgettable lessons and memories between us. Every trip also had its own element of adventure. Katie's trip, for example, happened at the start of a long bear market from 2000 to 2002. I don't like to be gone from the office traveling during bear markets. Since Katie graduated in 2000, I considered delaying her senior trip to another time.

"But Dad," Katie pleaded, "if we don't go *now*, we're never going to go!"

She was right. That bear market was hell. When it didn't look like it was ever going to end, I took a giant leap of faith and said, "Fine, this is a tough time for a senior trip, but we're going."

By visiting European internet cafes, even in the middle of the night, I stayed connected with our portfolios and was still able to celebrate Katie's high school graduation with her. But the situation wasn't optimal. Dicey internet connections just added to the stress of using physical maps in a foreign country; driving on the right side of the road at 120 miles per hour-plus on the autobahn; trying to figure out which exit to take while reading signs in a foreign language at high speed. Oh, the adventure of it! But my daughter was worth it.

It might not surprise you that Cathy's not a fan of adventure travel like these senior trips. She likes to go to Cancun and relax. We've spent many family vacations in Cancun, Cabo, and Hawaii. Making time for these many trips as a family gives us all an opportunity to decouple from work and chill. I schedule family time together like this as far in advance as I can—it's part of my overall goal to work nine months and take three months off throughout the year.

Besides traveling together, all three of my daughters have worked for me at some point, and all five of my children excel at whatever they do. They're talented, hardworking overachievers and leaders who make things happen. They're also competitive. My wife tells me, "You're the most competitive person I've ever met." But my wife is the most competitive person *I've* ever met! In fact, she was one of two starting running backs on her team in the 5A Division of Powder Puff Football at BYU.

One year, Cathy's University Villa women's football team won all their games, including the championship game against the Tribe of Many Feathers. But this rival team filed a complaint, saying one of the players on Cathy's team dropped out mid-semester, which disqualified them from winning the championship and getting the winning T-shirts! I chuckle about this now because Cathy has *never* let that injustice go!

As we've grown older, Cathy and I can now play some ping-pong or pickleball against each other, but when it comes to card or board games, we're all about winning. For example, after our honeymoon, when I first tried teaching Cathy to play Risk (where you try to take over the world by destroying the other player), that went sideways pretty quick. We had to stop playing competitive card or board games altogether. I don't know why. She's competitive; I'm competitive. It just doesn't work out. Our kids come by competition naturally.

Neither Cathy nor I have ever believed in the "everyone's a winner" program. We both know life isn't easy, so we taught all our kids that they had to be tough to excel. We didn't baby them at all. We also taught our kids that they could do anything they wanted as long as they were willing to do what it took to make that "anything" happen.

I believe families are extremely important and at the core of who we are. From personal experience, I know families are always complicated and always changing. In our family, Cathy and I have raised five children; we now have eleven grandchildren. Our children and their families have brought us some of the greatest joy of our lives. They've also taught us some of life's most important and sometimes difficult lessons. At any moment in any family's lives, it could be the best of times or the worst. During the worst, I think we can control whether we love unconditionally or not. I choose to love unconditionally.

Each member of your family is part of your life. It's up to you to figure out what that relationship means to you and what you're willing to work out with a family member. Earlier in this chapter I explained that a family portrait of us was just a snapshot in time. Likewise, the details I'm about to share about my children are just another snapshot in time. The rest of our family story is to be continued.

Shannon

A month before Cathy and I got married in June 1979, I graduated with a business degree from Brigham Young University in Provo, Utah. Shannon was born a year later in 1980. That year, while performing as a professional magician putting on 200+ "Grand Illusion" shows in large auditoriums throughout the Western United States, I realized the fun and financial success of being a magician would have to end. I was traveling so much, my one-year-old daughter didn't even recognize me! That's when I learned my family was more important to me than money or fame.

Still, I didn't give up my entrepreneurial spirit or my passion for hunting. In fact, Shannon was born on September 19, right in the middle of elk rut season. I was there for her birth, but I missed most of her birthdays. To make up for the missed birthdays, I've always scheduled a special date with her. We both always loved going on those special dates together. I also took Shannon on hunting trips with me. She tells me hunting was "fun" and that she loved everything about it—being in the mountains, hiking for miles, seeing incredible scenery—everything except getting the deer!

At three years old, Shannon started gymnastics. By the time she was twelve, she was practicing gymnastics five hours a day, four days a week to become a very good gymnast. Shannon has also always been an entrepreneur. At age eleven, she began teaching gymnastics to kids in the neighborhood using my camping sleeping pads. Once she started making some money, she put that money into legitimate gymnastics mats. Ultimately, she turned my garage into a gym covered with really nice mats. She'd teach up to thirty-five kids in her classes and used what she made from those classes to fund that stage of her life.

When Shannon injured her back as a junior in high school, she got talked into becoming a cheerleader, which other gymnasts looked down on. Although losing her gymnast identity was tough, Shannon turned into an amazing cheerleader who did all the cool tumbling and flips.

While working on a degree in public relations from BYU, she did a PR internship with For Every Body, a candle company. After graduating in 2005, she worked in New York City at a travel PR firm, Middleton and Gendron. Then she came back and worked full time at For Every Body. In 2007, she married Patrick Golladay in the Mount Timpanogos Temple. In November of that same year, Shannon went fishing with me on Strawberry Reservoir. She told me about all the ideas she had to grow Paragon and was excited to try some new things. "I'll put you on the map," she said. "How about you hire me?"

Why not? I thought, so I said, "Let's try it out for three months."

That's when I hired Shannon to do Paragon's PR. She started by creating Paragon's website and forced me to get on LinkedIn and Facebook. "You have to have it all, Dad, but I know you're not crazy about social media, so I'll be *you* on your social channels." Soon after she started writing back and forth to my friends like she was me, I started getting people telling me I had said something interesting online—but I didn't even know what it was! That was wild. About five years later, Shannon's husband wanted to get his MBA, so she stopped working for me. They moved to Arizona for the MBA, then to California where he worked for Wells Fargo, and now they're back home in Utah, where he's working for SoFi, a finance company that helps people "get their money right." Patrick and Shannon are a great couple.

After pregnancy, Shannon struggled with weight gain and depression. She didn't feel like herself. Through healthy nutrition, new types of exercise, supportive coaching, and her own personal determination, Shannon went from a size sixteen to a size six, which was smaller than she was in high school. She knew she wanted to work from home to take care of her three kids while helping other mothers do what she did, so she started her own business, Golladay Fit. By sharing her personal story of struggle and growth, other mothers relate to what my daughter has been through. She's super motivational and her website location describes who she is for others: YourPersonalCheerleader. com. I admire the online business Shannon has built. She's committed to raising her family and helping other women take care of themselves, so they can then take care of others.

Katie

Growing up, Katie was always a shy girl, which makes it amazing to see what a confident leader and speaker she's become now. She has always been a major practical joker. One time Katie took her younger sister Kelli to get her first massage. When Kelli went to the bathroom, Katie filled out her paperwork. When asked what Kelli's focus areas were, Katie wrote, "butt." Kelli had no idea going into her massage what she was in for!

Throughout high school, Katie played basketball and softball. She was always small but could hold her own and wouldn't take crap from opposing players. We nicknamed her, "Stands with a Fist," after the lead female character in *Dances with Wolves*.

Katie has cut my hair since 2002. She had been cutting hair for her guy friends in high school, so I took a leap of faith and let her start cutting mine in 2002 at the end of her cosmetology school.

Several years ago, Katie decided I should start coloring my hair, so I let her. Recently, I asked her, "When should I stop having you color my hair?"

"When you want to give up on life!"

Needless to say, Katie's still coloring my hair.

Katie married Byron Edwards on August 8, 2002, in the Mount Timpanogos Temple. We all loved Byron. He had a magnetic personality and worked for me as a trader doing research. Byron's Achilles, heel was migraine headaches. When he died unexpectedly at just twenty-six years old on October 21, 2005, Katie suddenly became a grieving single mother with a three-month-old daughter, Kali. Hundreds of people attended Byron's funeral, filling an entire LDS Stake Center.

This unimaginable loss blew up my daughter's life. As a father and grandfather, it was the first time I ever thought, "This is devastating. There's nothing I can do about this. I've just been handed something I can't fix, and I've always been able to fix anything." That realization was a turning point in my life. Eventually, the experience taught me that we're all going to be given different trials in life. As long as they don't destroy you—as long as you do whatever you can to *make sure* they don't destroy you—they'll build your character.

So now what?

Many people told Katie how having a child made her situation much more devastating; this bothered her. Katie's daughter actually gave her purpose and a reason to get up each day, even though a massive part of her just wanted to dig a hole, stay in it, and never come out. She attended therapy and had a great support system among family and friends.

Even though she wasn't sure she could handle college, a year after Byron died, Katie mustered the courage to take two classes, found out she *could* do college, and then plowed through a four-year degree in business and psychology in just two and a half years. College helped Katie pull out of her depression. While there, she felt the hardship of taking care of a child while going to school. Katie thought about what other widowed or divorced single moms, who didn't have the kind of emotional and financial support that she had, would be going through.

In 2010, when Shannon was still working for me, she came up with the idea of starting the Live Your Dream Foundation to provide scholarships for single mothers. Our family thought that was a great idea, so I worked with Shannon and Katie to set up the foundation. Shannon did the heavy lifting to get the all-volunteer foundation off the ground. Then she led it until she and her family moved to Arizona in 2011 when Katie took over. Since then, Katie has put her whole heart and soul into building the foundation organically over time. She spends forty or more hours of unpaid work a week growing the foundation. She and Devin Bunnell, her second husband, were married in 2008 and have had three children, who they're raising along with Kali.

Katie speaks to groups and the media regularly about the foundation's mission to support single mothers. Her current milestone goal is to raise $3,000,000. As of June 2023, the foundation has given out 240 scholarships, and Katie has helped raise over $880,000, so she's well on her way to reaching that milestone goal.

Our foundation's model allows donors to donate directly to the cause or support overhead costs. Because of Paragon's support and our volunteer structure, our overhead costs have been minimal. This structure enables us to both grow and give 100 percent to our cause. Since 2010, the foundation has given away hundreds of scholarships to single mothers in Utah. Another goal is to lift up those women most in need and give them the best shot possible to go to school, accomplish their goals, network with people, and move forward in life or effectively "Live Their Dreams!" It's very fulfilling to make such a difference and see their lives move forward in such a positive way.

On Utah Philanthropy Day in 2022, Katie was recognized as the Utah Philanthropy Outstanding Volunteer Award winner for 2022 by a committee of major philanthropic organizations in Utah.[1] Cathy and

---

1 Utah Philanthropy Day, "Honorees," https://utahphilanthropyday.org/honorees, accessed October 2, 2023.

I were proud to attend the ceremony on November 15 at the Hale Centre Theatre in Sandy, Utah, where they celebrated Katie's dedication. We now see a whole different version of our daughter than the shy little Katie she was as a kid.

Shawn

My first son, Shawn, is super smart and has always had a ton of friends. People in the neighborhood always said he was the kid who was most likely to become president. He graduated from Utah Valley University in business management. Shawn loves camping, the outdoors, and as you know from the stories I've told in earlier chapters, he's spent a lot of time hunting with me over the years. Shawn's a phenomenal skier, snowboarder, and wakeboarder. He's also an adventurous daredevil. If people were jumping off a forty-foot cliff at Lake Powell, Shawn would jump off a ninety-foot cliff. He's had ten concussions that he knows of for sure.

When Shawn was about nineteen, he started gambling and became very successful at it. Playing Blackjack in Wendover and Vegas, he could go out with $500 and come back with $15,000. I knew what was going on and was not happy about it. I kept warning my son about the dangers of gambling. Later I learned Shawn wanted to succeed and do bigger things than I'd done. For a while, gambling seemed to be working for him, but then it became a compulsion. Byron's death also hit Shawn hard.

When the kids were young, I established Roth IRAs for each of them so that when they were twenty, they'd have $20,000 to learn how to invest and grow. Unfortunately, money like that for someone with a gambling addiction can become a trap. The reason a compulsive gambler does seemingly stupid things like throw good money away, is that in their mind, they can't lose. Afterall, they've had a lot of success gambling. And since they believe they're going to win, they also believe they're just "temporarily borrowing" the money. This false belief leads to another false belief: *Borrowing this money's no problem because I'm going to pay it back.* Then when they can't pay it back, their addiction puts them in another box where they have no options. It becomes a vicious cycle. One of the consequences for individuals with a gambling disorder is being at risk for suicide fifteen times more than the general population.[2]

Once Shawn got access to his $20,000, he took it to Vegas and turned it into $45,000. So now he's got this wad of money and is leaving the casino when the guards stop him and say, "Hey, we'd really like to make you an offer to stay here." Then, even though my son is underage, they give him a top suite at the hotel and once again prove that casinos don't care about people; they just care about taking your money.

Meanwhile, Shawn's on top of the world in a fancy suite. Over the next couple of days, he gambles away the $45,000, including the original $20,000 from his Roth IRA. After that, he feels totally defeated and messed up, which is when he takes off driving way too fast in the desert west of Las Vegas without a seatbelt on. As the road turns, he continues to go straight off the pavement. Now airborne, he throws his fake ID out the window, yelling, "Here I come Byron!" Then his car flips five times into a ravine. Thankfully, a semi-truck driver sees that there has been an accident, grabs his fire extinguisher and puts out the flames. Then he notifies the police who life-flight Shawn to Vegas. We're all grateful to this truck driver and even more grateful that Shawn miraculously survived what could have been a deadly crash.

Shawn went on to build and manage a very successful home flipping business in Alabama. Over a period of four years, he bought and sold about sixty homes around Birmingham. Shawn's children and his relationships with those he loves are the most important thing in his life.

Kelli

When Kelli was born, she had reddish hair, so I teased Cathy, telling her, "Oh my gosh, we've got a hot-tempered little redhead!" As Kelli

---

2 Rob Davies, "Problem Gamblers at 15 Times Higher Risk of Suicide, Study Finds," *The Guardian*, March 12, 2019, https://www.theguardian.com/society/2019/mar/13/problem-gamblers-at-15-times-higher-risk-of-suicide-study-finds, accessed July 21, 2023.

grew older, her red hair became light brunette, but when she was little, I thought she was really small, so I teasingly called her "Ant Kelli." She didn't end up having a hot temper, but she's always had a lot of grit, which I admire.

Kelli told me her first memory as a child was flying to Disneyland with only me. I'd just had back fusion surgery and couldn't sit down, so the rest of our family drove while I took Kelli with me by plane because she was a free fare. We both stood in the back of the plane together holding hands. It's hard to believe she remembers this experience from when she was just two years old!

My youngest daughter and I think a lot alike. She's very smart, disciplined, logical, and a hard worker. She's also a gifted athlete, who once thought, incorrectly, that I was going to let her quit school and become a snowboard teacher! When I coached Kelli's Junior Jazz League basketball team in fifth and sixth grade, I built her team (and others) to win by focusing on each girl's specific strength. Kelli was short but quick, so she always played point guard, which continued into high school. She was a star athlete who played basketball and soccer through high school. She remembers me going to lots of her basketball and soccer games; I loved watching her play. She was recruited for both sports. Along the way, she broke her nose a couple of times, had some concussions, and dealt with several difficult sports injuries that led to her going into rehab for an addiction to painkillers.

Dixie State University (now Utah Tech University) in St. George, Utah, recruited Kelli to play soccer. In June, just two months before starting two-a-day training in the blistering August heat of southern Utah, Kelli had to have her gallbladder removed! Obviously, she's tough and determined. While at Dixie playing soccer, the cross-country coach noticed her speed and recruited Kelli to walk on to Dixie's cross-country team. She was their fifth fastest runner and earned the Dixie State University "Athlete of the Week." That was a big honor and happened during the NCAA regional races. She had run so hard during that competition and was doing really well until she literally passed out toward the end of the race from not drinking enough liquid, giving her a painful gravel rash.

After Dixie, Kelli went on to earn a degree in family finance from Utah State University in Logan. She says one of her favorite memories is when I dropped her off at Utah State in Logan. Kelli has worked as a mortgage broker, a tech recruiter, and for most of her career, an account manager at a few tech start-ups. In 2018 she married Peter Woods in the Draper Utah Temple. Peter is awesome. He earned a degree in communications and has worked in medical sales. I'm grateful that Peter has been so helpful to Kelli as she works to resolve her recent serious health issues and get her life back up to full speed.

Austin

By the time we got Austin, our fifth and final child, he was five years younger than Kelli. Without as many siblings around home, Austin was on his own the most. He's a real character—the class jokester and the epitome of making people feel comfortable. Austin's always got a smile on his face.

At Mountain View High School, he served on the student council as the class historian who put together the class video for graduation. All my kids are athletic, and Austin would have played basketball in high school, but he had a hip issue that kept him from that. Instead, he and his friend became the coleaders of the Bruin Crazies, a group of 300 to 400 kids who made up cheers, riled up the fans, and generally went crazy in the stadium during games. As one of the leaders, Austin would drape himself in this long garb, wear a brightly colored head-dress, and carry a stake like Moses.

During high school, my daughters were high achieving students, but my sons were more like me: they did what they thought mattered! Out of the whole crew of five kids, no one thought Austin would be the one to speak at graduation, but as the class historian, he got to speak in front of 3,000 + people, including dignitaries. Right off, Austin started telling stories and diving into controversies that the adults probably didn't want told, like how the refs made a mistake at a controversial football game and how the Bruin's had *obviously* won. Students thought he was hilarious; people in charge of graduation, not so much.

During high school, Cathy kept telling Austin, "You gotta go to college. You gotta go to college."

"Yeah, yeah," he'd say. "I'm gonna go to college. I'll figure it out."

Like Kelli, Austin went to Dixie for a couple of years, but then he stopped, which upset Cathy, of course. He decided he didn't like college; it was "a waste of his time."

After that, he founded and trademarked a company called IRBIN, which stands for "I'd rather be in nature." Spending as much time in nature as possible really defines who Austin is. He also started the #Idratherbeinnature hashtag. It's been used over 100,000 times on social media. Austin loves all things hunting, fishing, and camping. He's also one of only a few people who have flown a paraglider off Mount Timpanogos several times, the second-highest mountain in the Wasatch Range at 11,752 feet. Flying off a sheer, 500-foot cliff at the top of Timp is another level of hang gliding.

In 2019 a high school friend, Dover Janis, started a solar technology company based in San Diego, California, called Ivy Energy. Dover recruited Austin to do marketing for the company. He's always worked virtually from Utah and just got promoted to VP of marketing. Austin is very talented at making things happen. With all his amazing marketing activities, he's been a key player in growing Ivy Energy from a handful of people to an award-winning company with nearly fifty employees and growing.

Austin recently put Ivy Energy in for a prestigious Edison Award. The awards recognize top innovators and innovations from all over the world. Austin found out there were over 300 entries in their category. Even when he was told Ivy Energy had made it to the Top 100, he still didn't think they had a chance. Then they got an invitation to attend the gala in Fort Myers, Florida, where Thomas Edison's home is located. I helped Austin dig out one of his old suits just to be dressed appropriately for the black-tie event where he and Dover brushed shoulders with the who's who of venture capitalists and people like Pat Gelsinger (CEO at Intel) and Jonathan Ive (designer of the iPhone, iMac, and iPad).

Cathy and I learned by text that Ivy Energy had beat out all their competition and won the top award in the solar energy category! Then Austin texted pictures of himself and Dover holding the Gold in Critical Infrastructure for Virtual Grid, their innovative solar energy billing software. The software's proprietary algorithms enable property owners to invest in solar energy across multi-unit developments (not just single-family homes), and their tenants save money by getting access to green energy. "Owners can generate $500–$1,200 per unit in annual net operating income (NOI) on the Virtual Grid Platform, while tenants see savings of 10–15 % on their monthly energy bill."[3]

We've watched Austin go from this single, fun-loving, every-weekend-camping-with-friends guy to helping build a Greentech start-up. His work with green energy aligns with his love of the outdoors, where he's learned some of life's most important lessons. Austin has also literally spent hundreds of nights in the backcountry camping and hunting with me over the years.

He recently told me exactly what he learned when he, Kelli, and I hiked the Inca Trail in Peru to Machu Picchu. To complete his Eagle Scout project, we delivered 200 pounds of clothing and goods to remote villages in the Andes. Like Kelli, who said that our Peru trip was a "life changer," Austin said that trek taught him about "charity, hard work, and grit; determination against the odds, pushing through the pain and sickness; picking yourself up when you fall down, and giving it everything you've got."

Not surprising, Austin met his wife Brooke on a river rafting trip in Utah. From the way he and other guys were talking, Brooke thought Austin was a total player. Then they got to know each other better, and she changed her mind. Brooke loves the outdoors and flies off mountains like Austin using a paraglider. I had the privilege of marrying them in 2019, and now they have a house, a dog, chickens, a garden, and she gave birth to our eleventh grandchild, a boy, on June 14, 2023.

---

3 The Edison Awards™, "Edison Best New Product Awards™ 2023 Winners," https://edisonawards.com/2023-winners/, accessed August 24, 2023.

Value Your Friends

You probably have a core group of friends and many more acquaintances that come and go throughout your life. When I became the mayor of Orem, for example, a lot of people suddenly wanted to know me or be my friend.

People can be funny about how they interact with someone they perceive as famous or wealthy. And money is like a magnet for friends. I know a wealthy woman who gets treated like royalty. She's a nice, simple lady, but all these people fall down around her, believing people with money or people in politics are a big deal. I've never seen life like that. Titles don't mean much to me. I've always respected the person—not the title or the degrees. If I meet a bigwig, I want to talk to them as a person. I want people to see me as a person too. If I have to, I'll put down "mayor" after my name, but mostly, I just sign with "Dave."

When I was thinking about running for mayor, I asked each of my kids what they thought about it. They all had different opinions, but their overriding opinion was this: "Dad, you don't even like the limelight. Usually, you only talk to a few people you consider friends. Why would you want to be the mayor and have the spotlight on you?" I had to think a lot about the answer to that question before I decided to run.

Back in the day when I worked as a magician performing in Vegas and at university campuses all over the West, I'd put on magic shows in front of hundreds and sometimes thousands of people. After a performance, fans would ask for my autograph or a picture. They saw me as a kind of celebrity. A lot of people wanted to get to know me.

At the time, I was also earning a degree in business at Brigham Young University, so I'd get back to campus from a magic show road trip, wake up in the morning like everybody else, take a shower, throw on my backpack, walk all over BYU, and blend in—just like any one of thousands of students. I hadn't changed, but people's perceptions of me changed. In one scenario, I was a big deal; people wanted my autograph. In the other scenario, I was just the next guy in line.

When I talk about valuing your true friends, I'm talking about the people you can call on for anything, the people you have a real relationship with. They're the friends you know that regardless of what happens to you—if you're successful or not—they care about you. They want to hang with you, and you want to hang with them. I don't think you have tons and tons of those relationships. But they're the true friendships I encourage you to cultivate, value, and be grateful for.

My relationships with friends like these go back to when I was younger and had young children, hanging out with other young couples. Since my family has grown larger and grown up, though, I don't see these friends as often. But whenever I do, we're right back to the point when I last saw them, even though that might have been years earlier. I have a deep relationship with these friends. We care about each other; we trust each other; we're there for each other.

When I became mayor, the people I *really* knew had my back. Even some relationships with people I knew as just casual acquaintances had my back. In Chapter 10, I talk about living your legacy now. I also share about Nathan Ricks, a close friend of mine who was killed in a plane crash on January 3, 2023. He was just two years younger than I am. Losing him as a friend was rough. It reminded me, again, the value of true friends and how important it is to tell your friends, sooner than later, how grateful you are to them and how much they mean to you.

Value Your Community

In March 2021, several influential members of the community asked me to run for mayor of Orem, a city of 100,000 + people. I've always been involved in the background of Orem politics, and I've always been very much aware of the good and bad that goes on in our city. But I've *never* had a desire to run for political office.

When friends started pestering me to run, I'd tell them that I liked my current life and had no reason to run. Still, they kept pushing. "Orem is at a tipping point," they'd say. "Without good leadership, the city will continue down the path of continuously adding more high-density apartments without decent infrastructure, creating the traffic nightmare that Orem is becoming." I didn't disagree with them, but I still didn't want to run for mayor.

So they took another tack.

"A number of forces are pushing Orem away from its motto of 'Family City USA,'" they'd point out. "Without decent leadership, Orem will move completely away from the core values that have always made it a great place to live." I couldn't disagree with that either. I've lived and raised a family in the area for more than thirty years, back when it was all apple and peach orchards. Things were very different then. Cathy and I had to remove an old, abandoned school bus from our lot before we could build one of the first homes in the Countryside subdivision. Although I, too, wanted leaders who would direct city development according to our community's family-centered values, I was still resisting a run for mayor.

Then, after a month of me saying, "No, No, No," I suddenly got a strong feeling that I should consider running for mayor. Later in my book, I'll explain more about how we all have access to this sixth sense, or inner guidance, and how we can benefit from listening to our inner guide for ourselves and each other. In this case, a strong feeling caused me to begin contemplating what I, in particular, could do for Orem, a city that my wife and I care a lot about. Once I paid attention to this strong feeling and took time to reflect on how I had the experience, ability, and network to make a difference and get Orem back on track, I threw my hat in the ring on June 7, 2021 (the last day to enter the race), ran as an underdog, and won.

While becoming mayor surprised me, once I did, I organized my vision for the city of Orem into a plan that shows just how much I value my community. As Orem's mayor, I'm actively engaged in working through this plan to improve the quality of life for the people who live and work here.

For decades, I knew Orem had been a great place to live. But since about 2008, it started going sideways. Big developments brought in high-density apartments, increased traffic, and eroded the family neighborhoods that form the heart of Orem's structure and way of life. The Orem that I and so many of our fantastic residents love began to disappear. The big development mindset and approach to city growth got it wrong.

To halt that type of growth and ensure the city remains a great place for families to live, my first priority as mayor has been to protect our neighborhoods. After I was elected, one of my first wins was successfully changing the zoning laws on State Street. This change effectively prevented 10,000 apartments from being built along the city's main thoroughfare. This change moved the balance of housing options back to what our community actually wanted, effectively reversing the stranglehold developers had over Orem during the previous twelve years.

Another major priority was to change how the city government operates structurally. For some time, our mayor and Orem City Council had primarily acted in a ceremonial role while unelected Orem City staff dictated the direction of the city. After a lot of effort, we restored the city council to its proper role as the legislative body that guides and directs the city and is directly accountable to the will of the people. As a side benefit, we reduced our payroll costs by $1.1 million in the first six months of these changes.

In order to align the will of the citizens with the city council and city employees, we brought back the designation of Family City USA to Orem. Everything in Orem was rebranded, including city entrances, buildings, signs, public parks, and even our city flag. Most importantly, Family City USA is now the benchmark by which all city council legislative decisions are measured.

Including our new state-of-the-art City Center, three public parks, and our water conservation project, these five major infrastructure projects will cost about $100 million dollars. These projects will provide tremendous benefits to our community for the next several decades. Best of all, there will be NO TAX INCREASES as a result of any of these projects. But shifting the distribution of power in a city government is difficult. It takes patience, commitment, and hard work. No one likes giving up power, even when it's going to create a government that's more representative of the people and accountable in its decision-making process.

After a year and a half serving as mayor and spearheading these positive changes with the Orem City Council, I got tired of reading misinformation disseminated by some media outlets that was inaccurate, distorted the truth, or misrepresented our work. Toward the end of one city council meeting in September 2023, it felt like the right thing to do to set the record straight for the betterment of my city. In particular, I laid out a case against what a reporter at the *Daily Herald*, a small local newspaper, had been reporting and why they should stop. My remarks got a standing ovation. However, right after that meeting, I was physically attacked by the daughter of this reporter in the parking lot. Fortunately, I was not seriously hurt, and bystanders recorded the incident, which got a lot of media attention.[4]

My intention in bringing to light the long-standing issues with irresponsible reporting was to encourage people to rise above the divisiveness and misinformation overshadowing the amazing work of the city council. As a community, I know we are better than this, and I hope this incident will further serve as a wake-up call for the need for more responsible journalism and for each of us to work together with greater civility and unity. Truth can be distorted to the point where it becomes unrecognizable. It's scary, but that's just how it works. I've fought through any negative stories by keeping my vision for Orem front and center. Focus is key.

My background in finance and investments has been invaluable to this part of my mayoral responsibilities. By understanding and pushing back on unnecessary school district bonds, as well as finding grants from contacts at the county and federal levels, we have been able to save our taxpayers tens of millions of dollars. I've also learned about employee dissatisfaction and staffing troubles that can only have been the result of leadership failures. My background leading the Paragon Wealth Management team and evaluating various start-ups

---

4 Brian Mullahy, "Orem Mayor Assaulted on Camera After Council Meeting; Suspect Arrested," KUTV, September 20, 2023, https://kutv.com/news/local/orem-mayor-david-young-assaulted-after-city-council-meeting-suspect-linnea-pugmire-arrested-spit-on-public-official-provo-daily-herald, accessed October 2, 2023.

has also been essential to understanding why parts of how Orem's city government operates needed to change.

This is my vision for a city I love and am privileged to represent and serve. In Chapter 10, I'll talk more about what we've accomplished in Orem so far to show you one example of how and why to live your legacy now.

The Quality of Your Life

While writing this book, I started looking closely at where I put my focus during any given week. Here's one example from a typical week in the life of a mayor, financial advisor, big game hunter, and family man:

- Apply for and set up for deer hunts in New Mexico and Colorado.
- Work through and figure out major tax issues before April 15.
- Work with attorneys to file written arguments to the Alabama Supreme Court suit.
- Write and record Orem video message.
- Write Paragon newsletter.
- Engage in a major zoning battle to change and protect all parks and schools permanently.
- Work on a chapter draft of *Hunting for True Wealth*.
- Book fall family trip to Cancun.

This bulleted list from one week in April 2023 shows how what you focus on can directly affect the quality of your life and your happiness. I recommend living your life based on the things that you can impact and control: Your plans, dreams, and goals. Your relationships. Your experiences. Your faith. Whether or not you choose to be offended. Whether or not you choose to have a good day. Whether or not you see the beautiful world around you rather than the problems of life. How you react to the challenges that come into your life. Your attitude.

Likewise, when it comes to financial investments, what can you control? What level of risk are you willing to take? Are you taking too little or too much risk? Do you have a solid investment plan in place?

Are you sticking to your budget? Do you have an estate plan? Are you giving compound interest time to work for you?

Now consider the opposite: What affects your life but is completely out of your control? What's said on television. Comments on social media from the MPC (Miserable People's Club). The movement of the financial markets. Politics. People who disagree with you. People who complain about everything. The weather. Random bad things that happen to good people. Taxes. Whether or not you get sick. When you die.

Instead of focusing on things you can't control, focus on gratitude. Focus on giving to causes where you can make a difference. Have a victor rather than a victim mentality. And remember: Focus on those things you can control. Equally important: Most people are fundamentally good. Spend your time with good people.

CHAPTER 5

HUNTING WHITETAIL DEER IN IDAHO

I n my early thirties, I went whitetail deer hunting with my buddy Rich Lowe near the Clearwater River in Idaho. The nearest city was Grangeville. Two years prior, a man from Orem had drowned on a bear hunt in the same area.

By this time, I had several years of experience under my belt—but nowhere near the judgment and instincts that I have today.

We'd been out in the wilderness for a handful of days and, one morning, decided to split up. The November air had a refreshing chill to it. I made my way up to the top of a mountain plateau that overlooked the river. The jungle-like foliage was thick, so I couldn't just walk through it easily. Deer had beaten down some narrow trails through the vegetation, so I was using one of those trails, but not without effort.

All of a sudden, as I made my way through the heavy brush, this buck appeared right in front of me. Maybe that's why they call hunting whitetail "hunting ghosts." He was standing just twenty-five yards away from me and to the right. Instinctively, I swung my gun around, aimed in the general direction, and took a straight-on shot—not my favorite. He didn't die instantly, which is unusual; I always hope to kill animals on the first shot. But scopes are made for shooting out a hundred yards. At twenty-five yards, I couldn't get the buck in my scope properly. The shot just injured the deer, pushing him backward.

Immediately after that, he looked at me, lowered his head, and charged full speed toward me on the same narrow trail we had both been using that morning. I had to jump into the brush to avoid getting impaled by his antlers. The whole experience—seeing him right on top of me at twenty-five yards away, then shooting him, then having him run straight at me and me having to get out of his way so he couldn't kill me—was intense. I've never had a deer charge me and try to take me out like that before.

I watched as the deer kept running and then dropped off the side of the mountain. *He's hit,* I thought, *and that sucker tried to kill me! I'm going after him.*

The steep but navigable incline must have been 1,400 feet down to the river below. I went over the side after the deer, following his blood trail. It felt like dropping into a Vietnamese jungle; the green foliage was so rich and dense. Ferns came at me from every direction; slippery moss covered everything; and I could barely see through the canopy above.

Following a blood trail can be very difficult. Depending on where you hit the animal, lower or higher on the body, it might bleed more or less. If it's a deep red blood, you've likely gut shot it. If you see bright red blood with bubbles in it, you've hit the lung.

The blood I found had a bright red hue, which meant I'd gotten a good lung shot and just needed to find the deer. I kept descending, and descending, and descending after it. This buck stayed mobile for a long time.

Three hours later, I reached the Clearwater River at the bottom of the mountain. I only had about thirty minutes of daylight left. Rich had probably already returned to camp.

The Clearwater River is about 120 feet across. On the other side of it, I could see a dirt road that I thought might be my best route out of the area. My only other option would be to turn around and try to climb back up the steep mountain.

All right, what am I going to do? I asked myself. *Climb back up, or cross the river?*

A more mature hunter wouldn't have done what I did.

I decided to cross the river. It had a healthy current, and with misguided confidence, I thought it looked manageable. I guessed that the water would reach my chest at the middle of the river.

Strapping on my backpack and rifle good and tight, I waded in. The water reached my knees. I could feel the current moving, but nothing worrisome.

Okay, I got this.

Pretty soon, the water reached my hips and started pushing me more and more. I still had two thirds of the river to cross. The ground kept dropping beneath me. By the time I had almost reached the halfway mark, the water had risen to my chest.

If I can just get past the halfway, I thought, *then I'll start going up the other side. I'll be fine.*

That northern Idaho November chill had been welcome during my march down the mountain, but now it put me at risk. The water was extremely cold. I could feel my temperature dropping, and I knew if I got too cold, hypothermia would be an issue.

This might not have been my best decision. I started second-guessing myself. But by that point, my options were limited.

I took another step. The ground disappeared beneath me.

Oh, shiz, I thought.

Grappling for my bearings, the current swept me down the middle of the river. My gear had gotten completely waterlogged and dragged at me. I tried to swim and keep making progress to the other side. I knew hypothermia would set in if I didn't get out of the water soon. Then I'd really be screwed. Hypothermia makes you lose your ability to do anything. I would drown.

That's when I started chanting in my head, *Don't panic. Don't panic. Don't panic. Don't panic.*

The whole time I struggled to stay oriented, swim the second half, and find the bottom of the river, I just kept repeating that mantra: *Don't panic.* Because if you panic in the backcountry, that's when you go in the wrong direction and get lost; that's when you get injured; that's when you drown or get attacked by a predator; that's when you die. As soon as you panic, you forfeit most of your viable options.

Even though I'd made the wrong decision to cross the river, I had enough experience—and good instincts—to develop and listen to that internal dialogue telling myself not to panic.

It came to me automatically. *Don't panic, don't panic, don't panic.*

And that's been my approach to any number of stressful situations in life. Just don't panic. When you panic, you start to make bad decisions—or compound bad decisions you've already made. If you don't panic, you can think the situation through, you can take it apart, make a plan, and take it one step at a time.

While keeping myself as calm as possible, I free-floated about 300 yards down the river. I could tell the moment I started losing it from onset hypothermia. My mind fogged, and thinking became a lot more difficult. Experiencing hypothermia feels like getting the life sucked out of you. Drowning in ice-cold water was turbo-charging the hypothermia. I felt hopeless, screwed. *Oh shiz*, I thought again. *Why did I try to cross this river*? *I don't have to be in this situation*! *What was I thinking*? All my options felt like they were quickly disappearing. My mind was going foggy; I was having a hard time thinking. The only thing I could think about was survival. I was being washed along in a very strong current, knowing I'd die if I couldn't get myself out of this water.

I came to a bend in the river, bringing me a bit closer to the far side. I grabbed a thick branch that was poking out over the water and hoped it wouldn't break. Pulling myself hand over hand along the length of it, I finally heaved myself up onto a patch of marshy riverbank.

I collapsed and passed out.

Right as I pulled myself out of the river, a pickup truck with some local hunters in it came down that dirt road and saw me. They ran over, picked me up, carried me to their truck, cranked up the heater, and started pulling off my soaking clothes. I don't remember any of it. I was out of it and don't remember what any of them looked like or said. When I came to, shivering and teeth chattering, I was buried under a threadbare blanket, a jacket and sweater, even a tarp, as they tried to warm me up with the truck heater blasting. I would have died if they hadn't come along.

The deer got away, of course, although I'm sure he died and ended up food for another predator. The circle of life.

Ultimately, I lived—and gained a valuable experience about staying calm amid a life-threatening situation, which made me a better hunter, a better investor, a better leader, and a better father.

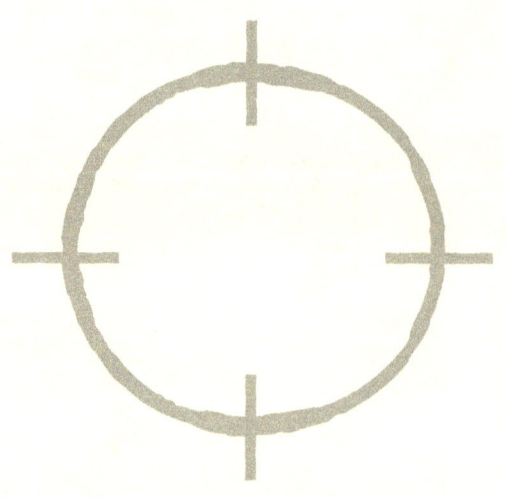

CHAPTER 6

DON'T PANIC; THINGS GO WRONG

Almost dying puts a lot of things in perspective. Chief among them is that things go wrong. That's life. You can follow all the right steps to build financial wealth. You can build solid foundations and relationships. You can be at the top of your game.

Things will still go wrong.

Sometimes life throws you curveballs that you don't see coming and strikes blows to your confidence, security, or happiness. The death of my son-in-law, Byron, was one of the first times in my life that I felt truly out of control. The lives of my daughter and granddaughter were upended. The loss was devastating for all of us, and *I couldn't fix it*.

Other times you make what you think is a good decision that ends up being a mistake or having consequences you didn't expect. I certainly didn't expect my decision to cross a river that looked totally navigable would lead to a near-death experience.

You will never find true wealth without accepting that you can't control everything, that you will never be perfect, and that you will never have a perfect life. How you react when things go wrong determines whether or not you will find true wealth.

This is the third principle you have to follow to hunt for true wealth and find deep happiness and success: Don't panic.

When things go wrong, when you lose control, the worst thing you can do is panic. As I explained in the previous chapter about hunting whitetail deer on Clearwater River, panicking provokes bad decisions—or it compounds bad decisions you've already made. If you can stop yourself from panicking, you carve out space to think through the situation. When you can think clearly, you can take the situation apart, make a plan, and take it one step at a time.

For some people, being able to remain calm in stressful situations is an innate talent they're born with. For other people, they've got to learn how to not panic. They've got to cultivate this mindset and response to stressful situations *like a skill*.

In this chapter, I explore four ways that you can incorporate the third principle of true wealth into your life: learn from your mistakes, listen for your inner guide, chase your edge, and find reminders to be grateful. As you read, think of this principle as a skill that you've got to learn or nurture alongside any other skills you value in your professional or personal life. Also consider how the other four principles of true wealth—go big or go home, build solid relationships, expect bear markets, and live your legacy—all serve to help you remain steady and not panic during life's struggles. Don't forget, there's no growth and no true wealth without struggle.

Learn from Your Mistakes

I firmly believe you can never hear this advice enough: Learn from your mistakes.

I've told anyone who will listen (my family, friends, employees) over and over: Learn from your mistakes.

Mistakes are growth opportunities. Handling mistakes properly is what separates those people who will succeed, grow, and find happiness from those who will *let themselves down*.

The wealthiest people in the world have all made mistakes, and plenty of them. You're not alone. Mistakes don't make you a failure.

In the following story, you'll see how I dealt with making a mistake that I thought was devastating, but actually made me a better hunter.

Hunting the Perfect Buck in the Mountains of Utah

By the time I reached twenty-five years old, I'd been hunting for a number of years and killed several deer. I was experienced and knew what I was doing—or so I thought.

My friend Richard King and I headed to Kanosh, Utah, to hunt deer. With its abundance of mountain ranges, Utah has some of the best hunting in the country.

On this hunting trip, we camped out at the base of a mountain, woke up before daylight, and climbed up into some high mountain basins. The morning passed well, if uneventfully. Rich and I split up, hiking away from each other.

Walking along the top of a narrow, ridge-like plateau that dropped off sharply on both sides, I was getting bored. It was approaching eleven o'clock in the morning; the best hunting was over. I started tossing rocks, pushing a boulder or two over the sides, making noise, hoping to spook something out of the ledges below me. After tumbling a boulder down the incline, I realized it didn't sound quite like a regular falling rock. It sounded like something running, so I hurried over to the edge of the plateau and looked down. A deer had gone all the way down the side of the ridge, across the narrow canyon floor, and up the ridge opposite me. It was directly across from me, running like a bat out of hell. About 350 yards separated us.

This deer remains, to this day, the biggest buck I've ever seen. A typical buck is twenty-four inches wide; this deer was about thirty-six inches. He was gigantic, with points going everywhere. If you don't know already, points are the individual tines on a buck's antlers. The more points a buck has, the better it scores—making it a more impressive trophy.

The lower end score for a trophy buck is around 180 inches. With the mass, width, height, and points on its antlers, this buck would easily score 240 or 250.

Holy shiz! I thought. This was what hunters dream of.

Raising my gun, I got on the buck, keeping it in my sights as it climbed the ridge. It moved *fast*, but I followed it. Right as I squeezed off, it turned, zigging instead of zagging, climbing in the opposite direction. The bullet hit right where the buck would have been if it had continued its original direction.

I got this, I thought as I got right back on the buck. I was free-handing, no dead rest, but I still felt confident I had it. Spooked even more now, the buck was racing full speed.

I squeezed off another shot.

Same thing happened. In the millisecond before my bullet hit the side of the ridge, the buck turned.

With almost no pause, I squeezed off a third time.

Again, the buck reversed course!

It was like divine intervention in favor of this animal. My aim wasn't the problem. If it had continued the same path, I would have hit it. And it wasn't like the animal could move faster than a speeding bullet. No, somehow it turned, three times, right in the nick of time.

I knew I only had one more chance before it disappeared over the top of the ridge. I squeezed the trigger. My last shot hit *right below the buck*, just as it bailed over the top and out of sight.

I plopped down on the ground and dropped my gun beside me.

Not okay, I thought, pissed. I'd been beaten by the biggest buck I'd ever seen in my life.

Up until then, I had killed nine deer with only ten bullets. No misses. And then this massive buck came along.

I was devastated. It felt similar to panic—this sudden overwhelming and uncontrollable fear that I had no clue what I was doing as a hunter, and all my time practicing had been for nothing. I'd just let the biggest deer I'd ever seen get away because of a completely avoidable error. By then, I had hundreds of hours of hunting experience under my belt, hiking in mountains, under the exact same conditions. At 350 yards, I should have known I needed a dead rest to execute this shot. But at crunch time, I didn't execute.

Looking back on it, I could see my rookie mistake. I should have taken more time to get my sight set. Taking four shots was way too many without a dead rest (a stable, unmoving shooting position). Then I repeated that same approach to my shot four times, instead of making adjustments in response to what I was observing in the moment (my misses and the deer's behavior). But I let my excitement and adrenaline pull me along. In a perfect world, I would have given myself more time, stabilized properly, taken a deep breath and relaxed, waited for that perfect shot, and killed the buck with one shot. That was completely doable.

Going forward, I never made that mistake again.

For six to twelve months following that hunt, every time I'd go for a walk or find myself in between activities, I'd play the entire sequence back in my head. I dissected what I should have done, over and over, not to beat myself up, but to know what I had to do the next time I was in that situation. I replayed what happened, and then I replaced it with the correct actions I should have taken.

That's how you train yourself not to panic. Learn from your mistakes. Replay them, dissect them, and take corrective action. Assume things will go wrong, no matter how good you are, and don't let yourself be paralyzed by fear, panic, or doubt. Perfection is a pipe dream. Even with my track record up to that point (nine deer with only ten bullets), I hadn't yet learned to expect that something would go wrong or that mistakes would still happen, no matter how much experience I had under my belt. Today, in all areas of my life, I assume things will go wrong and that I'll make mistakes. What I first experienced as a devastating failure turned into an opportunity where I demanded growth of myself—because no way was I going to let myself down.

Listen for Your Inner Guide

Listening and learning to listen is one of the thirteen values of true wealth. When you follow the seven steps that I set out in Chapter 2 for building financial wealth, you're listening to expert advice. You're also hearing part of my story, as an expert in investing, that I spent thirty-seven years writing, experiencing, and then telling. The stories and experiences I share are honest; they're a part of me. And by sharing them with you, I expand my impact beyond myself and bridge a gap between us. The same is true of Chapter 4, where I share the principle of building solid relationships.

Listening to the people around you—either friends and family you love or professionals you respect and need for their expert guidance—is essential to cultivating the ability to stay calm when life gets tough. Being able to actively listen and hear what other people are telling you, whether you agree with them or not, whether you decide to follow their advice or take a different route, leads to greater learning, wisdom, self-awareness, and self-confidence. It also helps you feel supported and connected to the people around you, which will help you combat panic whenever you might experience stress, hardship, and loss of control.

Equally important to not panicking is learning to listen *to yourself*.

A lot of my life has been about doing the opposite of what people say I should do. True wealth simply isn't possible if all you do is follow other people or try to make them happy. Independence and freedom, for example, two other values of true wealth, ultimately have to come from within you. By learning to listen to yourself, the calm, focus, and self-control that you create don't depend on anyone or anything external to yourself. *That* is independence and freedom. In the following story about hunting deer, this time in Wyoming, I show you the power of your inner guide and why you should listen.

Hunting Deer on the Greys River in Wyoming

I've spent a ton of time out in the mountains. Hunting typically takes place during the first and last hours of the day, since that's when most of the animals you're looking for are active. After the morning hunt, they start bedding down in the trees and disappear until early evening.

During midday, hunting becomes harder and more of a mind game. The gaps between when you spot animals get wider, making patience and commitment essential. That's also when you might climb up a steep incline to get a better vantage point with an unobstructed view into the trees on the other side of the mountain. In the right context, like in the mountains above Kanosh, Utah, you start early glassing for hours and hours. Then later in the day when you're getting kind of bored, you might even try to flush out animals by rolling rocks off a cliff and making noise.

After I had a significant amount of hunting experience under my belt, I noticed something interesting. On many of my hunts, I'd be passing a completely normal afternoon looking for that atypical animal not practicing the same bedding behavior as its fellows. Nothing would appear out of the ordinary for several hours. No disturbances in my surroundings at all.

Then, all of a sudden, I'd start to feel like I was about to see the animal I was hunting. It would be a very strong feeling, a sixth sense. Sometimes I think it's what knowing the future must feel like. More often than not, within five minutes of getting that feeling, the animal would appear—and usually a good one at that.

That feeling was never stronger than when I hunted deer on the Greys River in Wyoming. On this fall hunt in 2001, it knocked me over the head like a club.

The Greys River is a rushing mountain tributary that flows between the high Wyoming Range to the east and the Salt River Range to the west. Many know it as the starkly beautiful Wind River area.

By this time, I had entered my forties. I went on the hunt with my son Shawn, another hunting buddy named Richard King, and his boys. We spent several days hiking, searching, and glassing without finding any worthwhile bucks.

In the middle of the afternoon on the fourth day, that feeling, that sixth sense, suddenly hit me. It stopped me in my tracks. Because I had taught myself not to dismiss or ignore that feeling, I knew I wasn't alone. Bringing my rifle up in anticipation of what might happen next, I went on high alert and became extremely aware of everything around me. Adrenaline coursed through me, and I concentrated on keeping my breathing even. This type of response comes from the same place inside you where panic lives. But one leads to hyper-focus and excellence in action, while the other leads to bad decisions, emotional turmoil, and unhappy experiences.

The next thing I knew, a deer busted out of the trees about fifty yards in front of me, running full speed. I found the deer in my scope and pulled the trigger right before it disappeared back into the forest.

Hiking over, I found it dropped in its tracks. For a few moments, I just stood there thinking, *Wow*.

I had that feeling. I saw the buck. I shot the buck.

Now, it's important to recognize the difference between an inner guide and raw emotion. In the world of finances, having a feeling about an investment isn't sufficient to justify pursuing it. If the data back it up—whether that's from quantitative financial analysis or years of experience understanding the markets—then a great investment can certainly start from the kernel of a gut feeling. But what I'm talking about in this hunting story, and that pattern I realized had emerged over many years of hunting, is deeper than having a good feeling about something.

One aspect of hunting true wealth is about listening to your heart, your inner voice, your inner guide. It's about cultivating that capacity to listen over time until you have full trust *in yourself*. In the context of financial investing and entrepreneurship, my inner guide has brought any number of potentially fantastic opportunities to my attention. Just like I suddenly knew when to go on high alert during my Greys River hunt, your inner guide can tell you when to sense opportunity, possibility, and change in the markets or your business landscape. But I never rely on that guide alone when making financial or business decisions. If I did, it would just be a feeling, separate from research, due diligence, and market experience.

Listening to your inner guide is also about doing those things that you have strong feelings of certainty about because they're the *right* thing to do. It won't always be something you *want* to do. You have to be able to distinguish between getting excited about a trend or hunch and knowing in your heart when something is your true path, your future, something you're meant to do.

Before becoming Mayor of Orem, for example, I had that same sixth sense. An incredibly strong, overwhelming feeling that I should run for election came out of nowhere. It hit me *after* I had already said no half a dozen times when friends and other community members asked me to run. We all believed that Orem had been going in the wrong direction for the last decade. Our small city had been taken over by high-density developers, and they were taking it down a path that the general public didn't want. If I didn't run, Orem would become much less of a family-friendly place to live.

Of course, before I officially decided, I did my due diligence and explored the feasibility of an election run. Because I had invested in and been involved in all kinds of commercial development projects, including multi-family development projects, I knew how to deal with developers. My community knew that with my experience, I'd stand up for family values and push back against developers. Although I didn't want to run for mayor, once that feeling started, I couldn't get rid of it. And nothing in my exploratory research gave me a reason why I shouldn't run—no matter how much I wished otherwise. A voice inside my head kept telling me, *You've got to do this*. It told me that *not* serving my community would be on me, and if I didn't try, I was being irresponsible because, rationally, no one would sign up for this job.

Holding public office is very tough when you actually want to do a good job and affect positive change. The politics that come with the role are brutal. Only narcissists would subject themselves to politics just for the ego of it. I finally gave in to the voice inside and became the mayor of Orem, Utah, a leadership role I never sought and never expected. But I'm glad I listened to that voice and have the responsibility and opportunity to lead the city in a new direction.

Reminding myself that my inner guide led me down this path helps me keep calm when those politics get out of hand. I know that I'm doing this for a reason, even when elements of it feel suffocating. Not only will listening to your inner guide make you less likely to make mistakes, but also when you do get into stressful situations, you'll be more likely to come out the other side of your experience intact, without regret.

The inner guide I encourage you to listen for is separate from you. It comes from somewhere else, wherever you believe that might be. It's not simply raw, undirected emotion. Your inner guide means the difference between panicking and hunting for true wealth. Teach yourself to listen to it. Let your inner guide lead you to trust and believe in yourself. Learning to listen to your inner guide is essential to cultivating the ability to remain calm and not panic when your stress and adrenaline levels go through the roof. It will serve you no matter what situation you find yourself in—a life-and-death situation while big game hunting, an investment opportunity that could have big ramifications for your finances, a business or entrepreneurship idea that could create fantastic growth (or flop disastrously), or a public-facing role in your community with politics that you surely could do without.

Chase Your Edge

At some point in our lives, we all experience the terrifying feeling of teetering right on the *edge* of panic. You do everything you can to hold yourself back, to push it away, to draw on all your strength to survive and stay on the right side of that edge. But many of the values of hunting for true wealth are all about embracing that terrified feeling and reveling in that edge. Adventure. Living in alignment. Fitness and health. Freedom. Born ready. Vision.

True wealth is not possible without taking risks (remembering that risk looks different for everyone). And with risk comes the possibility of panic. But once you accept that risk and the possibility of panic are natural, you can use them to grow. You can transform them into wealth. In the following story about whitewater rafting in the Grand Canyon, I help you see panic in a new and more useful light.

Whitewater Rafting the Monster Grand Canyon Rapids

In 2018, I took an incredible trip to the Grand Canyon. This was my third visit; I put it together with family friends and also brought my five kids, then ages twenty-four to thirty-seven. I wasn't convinced it was the best idea, but Katie even came while pregnant. What a great experience. It felt simultaneously like old times and new. Going on an extreme adventure with my adult children was something I'll never forget.

To begin the trip, my kids and I hiked fourteen miles down into the North Rim, also known as the "other side" and much less frequented part of the Grand Canyon. At the end of the hike, we met up with the rest of our party at Phantom Ranch, a lodge at the bottom of the Grand

Canyon on the north side of the Colorado River. It can only be reached by mule, foot, or river raft.

Once we were together (all sixteen of us!), we spent eight days exploring side and slot canyons, whitewater rafting, and spending time with each other. Our longest hike was a twenty-two-mile round trip from the bottom of the Grand Canyon up to Mooney Falls, a towering waterfall more than 200 feet tall on the Havasupai Indian Reservation, and back down again. That sounds backbreaking, but it was nothing compared to the more than 100 miles we rafted. We had five rafts, and each raft held three to four people.

The Grand Canyon's Colorado River rapids are among the biggest in the United States. Most rapids are rated on a scale of one to six. The Grand Canyon has its own scale that goes from one to ten. It's like riding a roller coaster or a bucking bronco. There's a real danger of drowning if you aren't skilled or strong enough.

My son Austin got thrown from his raft at the Hermit Rapid, which has some of the largest waves in the entire canyon. My other son, Shawn, was tossed from his kayak at the very steep Granite Rapid. The current held him under water for almost two minutes. The current pushed my own raft down the "bad side" of the Bedrock Rapid, where the river shoots through a narrow channel studded by rocks. Then, on our very last day, my raft flipped at the top of the Lava Falls Rapid. We had no choice but to swim the entire rapid; it was incredibly intense.

At the end of the trip, we helicoptered out of the bottom of the canyon with our gear. We had all learned how big, gnarly, and scary those rapids are firsthand. Like big game hunting, that trip of a lifetime was perfect for understanding the hunt for true wealth.

As we floated down the Colorado River, I was struck by the similarities between the river, life, and investing. Sometimes the river is smooth, pristine, and peaceful—much like the markets. Markets are easy to navigate when things are smooth; you just show up and make money. Our optimism (another value of true wealth) tells us that things are usually good...until they aren't. That's when the real test begins.

About the time you start to take the river for granted, you hear a rapid in the distance. Your adrenaline spikes as it approaches. Once you hear it, you know your options are limited. There's no turning back, and there will be no do-overs. For better or for worse, you're going down that rapid.

If it's a big rapid, and the riverbank or rock wall is within reach, you tether your raft, climb up, and scout the rapid ahead. You try to determine the best path through the rapid, which you know, deep in your core, will be unbelievably challenging. You will have to flawlessly and forcefully row against the current to make it through the rapid safely.

So you tighten the straps on your life jacket. If the rapid is especially intense, with froth and whirlpools, you even add a second life jacket. Next, you put on your helmet. Finally, you remove your tether, push off, and head back toward the rapid. Everything crystallizes. Life narrows to its purest form. You do everything you've been trained to do and hope for a little luck to boot. As you start to slide over the top into the rapid's waves, you mentally cross your fingers that your oarsman and the other people in the raft know what they're doing.

When you're in the thick of a whitewater rapid or a tanking market, it's not the time to panic and change plans. You survive both by following a preplanned, stress-tested, systematic strategy. (For building wealth, review the seven steps I laid out in Chapter 2.) By understanding the nature of the river—that sometimes it's smooth and peaceful, while other times it churns and whips around like a giant washing machine's spin cycle—you can acknowledge a fundamental fact of life: panic, without preparation, is inevitable. Once you acknowledge this, you can work to prevent panic—and you can even start to find the thrill in it, without giving into it. Both aspects of the river are natural. Or, both aspects of the river are miracles and monsters of nature. Life would be incredibly boring without them.

Adventure, and pursuing activities like big game hunting and whitewater rafting, allows you to find your edge. It allows you to run right up against the edge where panic starts and control stops. Every one of the sixteen people on those rafts in the Grand Canyon had to confront their own edge. By doing this slowly, you'll push that edge back farther and farther, expanding your scope of control and evolving what risk means to you. Don't shy away from your edge. Chase it across your entire lifetime. Step right up to it. Embrace your discomfort and make your edge serve you.

Find Reminders to Be Grateful

Being able to get up, go out into the world, and have experiences that push us to grow is a miraculous thing. Even when those experiences are stressful or painful, they're worth our appreciation and gratitude. Finding reminders to be grateful will help you weather stress, risk, negativity, and panic. This is why gratitude is a value of true wealth. It's an antidote to the parts of life that we can either let poison us or use to hunt for true wealth.

In Chapter 5, I told you about a near-death experience I had on the Clearwater River. To close this chapter, I'm going to share another experience where I almost died. This time, it had nothing to do with hunting or the dangers of the back country. This story hits much closer to home.

A Near-death Experience in the Hospital

Let me tell you about the time the folks at a hospital tried to kill me. This was a frickin' nightmare.

During one Christmas season at the end of 2011, I had an emergency colectomy (bowel resection) surgery and spent about a month over the next year in and out of the hospital trying to recover. The surgical incisions were eight inches horizontal across my abdomen and ten inches vertical. The medical team said the surgery would take forty-five minutes, but it ended up lasting several hours. The surgeons took out some of my intestines and then put them back. They told me that because of the four holes I had in my colon from diverticulitis, my abdomen was full of poison, like when a person's appendix ruptures. An appendix rupturing is like having just one hole in your colon, but I had four (much worse).

The surgeons basically had to cut eighteen inches of colon and then reattach it as a colostomy, but they also had to move things around, which meant they took my insides outside my body, drained the poison by sucking it out, and took my appendix out (as long as they were there). Then they put it all back inside me before sewing me back up. When one of the surgeons went to the waiting room to update my wife, he was literally shaking. That doesn't inspire confidence. That's not the visual you want from your doctor after surgery.

Lying in recovery on Boxing Day, the pain was excruciating. I couldn't use any narcotics because I'd just had a knee replacement, and taking narcotics for that pain is what landed me in the hospital in the first place. The narcotics had shut down my digestive system. All I could take was Advil and Tylenol.

To add one more layer of difficulty, after the surgery, the doctors shoved a nasogastric tube up my nose and down my throat. Propped up in the hospital bed, relaxing was pretty much impossible. If I turned my head the wrong way, I couldn't frickin' breathe. And since it was the day after Christmas, all the good doctors and staff had taken the holiday off. Forget about the A-Team or even B-Team. I got stuck with the C-Team.

A physical therapist came into my room and announced, "Okay, we've got to get you up!"

With a tube down my throat, I couldn't talk. But I did my best to wave him off and say, "No!"

"Oh, we have to get you up," he kept saying. "That's the first thing we're supposed to do to get you going."

It must have been the first time he'd ever been put in charge. I felt like I had been cut in half; the pain was indescribable. I argued the best I could with a tube shoved down my nose and throat.

"I'm going to get a nurse, and she's going to come help me get you up," he said.

Together, they grabbed me. I tried to fight, but I had a tube down my throat, double surgical incision wounds, needles in both my arms, and no heavy-duty painkillers in my system. I had no control.

As they lifted me up, the movement pushed the tube sideways. I couldn't breathe or rearrange the tube. My panic was short-lived, though. Gagging and gasping, I passed out.

The next thing I knew, I was lying flat on the bed, and loud noises—a code being called and the monitoring machines sounding alarms—were going off all around me. A doctor ran into the room and, somehow, reached down my throat and grabbed the tube. He yanked the whole tube out, ripping away the top inside of my right nostril.

After they triaged my nose with gauze to stop the bleeding, I lay there in the bed stewing in my rage. I'm not an angry person, but this whole situation totally pissed me off. I felt like these medical "professionals" were trying to kill me.

While I lay there, covered in sweat, my family's stake president from church walked in holding a poinsettia. He gaped at me and asked, "Are you okay?"

"No," I said. "I am not okay." And I used every curse word I could think of. (For me, cursing is a great alternative to panic.) "These people are trying to kill me. This is unreal. You've got to get me help. You've got to get me out of here. You've got to stop this."

He looked down at the poinsettia. "This probably isn't helping, is it?"

No, I didn't need the poinsettia.

After that harrowing experience, every time I catch sight of my crooked nose, it reminds me to be grateful I'm alive.

So live your life to the fullest. Don't waste time worrying or shying away from stressful situations out of fear that you might panic. Things go wrong—in hospitals surrounded by people who are supposed to know what they're doing, or out in the middle of nowhere surrounded by predators and the elements. There's always a next nightmare waiting for you. Whether or not you worry, avoid tough situations, or do everything you can to *not* put yourself in a place where you might panic.

Panic doesn't only come after a shortsighted or bad decision, like crossing a freezing river or shooting four times at the biggest buck you've ever seen without making any adjustments. It can also make you run away from decisions that could be amazing for you, like the big investment that will pay out as soon as the markets rebound, or a business idea that could change your life if you commit to it. You can view mistakes, and that edge where control stops and panic begins, as the worst that life has to offer. Or you can view them as invaluable to hunting the best that life has to offer: true wealth.

CHAPTER 7

HUNTING MOUNTAIN GOAT IN ALASKA, THE FIRST TWO ATTEMPTS

In 2002, I made the first of two trips to the Takhin River Valley in Alaska to get a record book—quality mountain goat. On the first trip, my teenage son Shawn came with me. Shawn was all about hunting, but he was only seventeen years old at the time, so I had to get permission from my guide, Al Gilliam, for him to accompany us. It wasn't until we were flying into Juneau, Alaska, that I told Shawn he was coming along as my packer.

On a big hunt like this, you usually have a guide, a packer, and yourself. Shawn was excited to be my packer—the guy to help carry the 250-to-300-pound goat down the mountain.

Al was one of the few old breeds of guides who love the outdoors, know how to survive in extreme conditions, revel in the hunt, and want to help us hunters take a record-book animal.

"I'm sure we'll find some record billy goats way back in the valley," Al told me. "But harvesting one will take more effort than usual."

Any time you go after a trophy animal, you've got to get way back from civilization. You've got to go places where nobody else goes. That's where the biggest animals live.

"In a normal year, snow pushes the goats down the mountain," Al explained. "But this year it's barely snowed."

Story of my life. Here we are in the middle of November in Alaska, and there's no snow. That doesn't happen. But it did this year.

The three of us camped down at the bank of the Takhin River. Looking up through my spotting scope 4,500 feet above us, we could see the type of billy goats we were after—four of them. Their body size looked 30 percent bigger than normal, and the base of their horns was exceptionally heavy.

Those goats were our Goliath. They were survivors. They instinctively kept away from predators or any human movement. To get to them, you had to go where other people wouldn't go—either because it's too difficult or extreme, or it's just not worth it to them. Most trophy hunters won't go to places like this. They'll settle. But to get that record-book trophy, you can't just go where everyone else goes. You can't just follow the well-worn trails. You have to make your way into the backcountry where nobody goes. That's where you'll find the exceptional trophy animals you're looking for.

Over the course of this first hunt, we made three grueling, unsuccessful attempts to climb within range of the big goats, but we could never quite close the gap. The temperature went down to minus twenty degrees below zero at night. During the day, it would rise to fifteen degrees above zero. So we'd start before dawn and wade across the middle of the river filled with silver salmon. The water along the banks had iced over.

Once we got out of the river, we took off our waders and hung them on a tree, so some bear wandering by didn't take them. The waders would freeze solid before we returned; pulling them back on would be awful. For now, though, we put on our climbing gear.

To get away from the riverbank so we could start up the mountain, we first had to cut our way with machetes through more than fifty yards of thick, brambly underbrush. Winding through all that brush were nasty sticker bushes, devil's club, and wild rose. So even before we'd started up the mountain, we were covered in sweat with splinters in our hands that wouldn't come out when we dug at them.

"This is ridiculous!" Shawn said, as he laughed and caught his breath.

"No kidding," I said. "You got this big guy, we haven't even started!"

Coming out the other side of the brush, we began our ascent up the rockslides, working our way through thick alders and up the cliffs. Because the mountain was so steep, we had to find places to climb where water had come down in warmer weather, cutting out almost vertical ravines. We weren't taking a nice little hike up the mountain. We were climbing straight up with picks and ropes and fifty-pound packs. Sometimes rain, snow, and sleet slowed us down; other times the weather was clear. Our intent was to make the climb, locate and take a goat, and then descend.

But we didn't have enough gear to stay on the mountain for long. Every day for three days we had to re-climb 4,500 feet and try to get closer to the goats each time before being forced to come back down before dark—or else we'd get stuck on the cliffs.

Even though we moved as quickly as possible, it soon became apparent we were attempting the impossible. There just wasn't enough daylight to make it up and back down the mountain. We did have rain gear, but we were still soaked through with sweat from the exertion of the climb. And without overnight gear, we would freeze to death, so staying on the mountain wasn't an option.

When we left Alaska, Al offered to let us come back the following year at his cost. He felt really bad. We'd gone to all this effort, and he hadn't had us bring the right gear to be able to climb up the mountain, stay on the mountain, and continue hunting. Repeatedly going up and down was brutal.

I wanted to keep hunting to get what we came for, but Al's legs were wrecked. The tops of his climbing boots were so rigid that the pressure and rubbing as he climbed had dug deep lacerations into his calves all the way around them.

"I'm good, I'm good," Al kept repeating. "We're getting you that record."

Eventually, though, neither Shawn nor I could believe how he was managing to keep going. Al was a serious outdoorsman—tough as nails. Throughout those grueling nine days, there were several times when I wasn't sure I'd be making the flight home myself. But that was the adventure of it. Hardship. Hard work. Patience. Perseverance.

⟫━━━⟶

Within twelve months, I headed back to Alaska in 2003. This time Shawn couldn't come because of his first-year college program. I was scheduled to fly out of Salt Lake City, but our pilot's wife went into labor. His replacement showed up an hour later, but Delta decided he wasn't qualified. The third pilot brought in by the airline was late. I ended up missing all my connections and got stuck overnight in Juneau.

For all that trouble, Delta gave me a free five-minute phone card as compensation.

A day late, I finally made my way from Juneau to Haines, Alaska, in a four-seat airplane. At the river, I met Al and went by airboat as far up the river as we could, until we started running into huge log jams. We stopped, put on our waders, transferred our gear into a canoe, and started pushing and pulling it up the river against the current.

Maneuvering the canoe upriver in freezing cold glacier water and between frozen banks felt like walking through a field of slippery foot-diameter ball bearings. Just keeping our balance and staying out of the water was a project.

As it got dark, the temperature plunged. We unloaded the canoe and set up our bivouacs on the side of the river. A bivouac is a waterproof, cocoon-like sack that fits around and over your sleeping bag; ours were made of Gore-Tex. Up on the mountain, it's so steep we wouldn't have enough space to pitch a two-man tent.

Where we had to sleep that night put us on the main migration path traveled by grizzly bears that time of year. We saw fresh tracks and slept with one eye open, but fortunately encountered no bears that night. We spent half the following day continuing to work our way up the river against the current, using ropes to pull the canoe.

Finally, we reached our destination and spent the rest of the day setting up our base camp on the river, glassing the mountain above us for goats, and preparing our gear for the ascent. For a second year in a row, not enough snow had fallen to push the goats down the mountain.

"No drinking water where we're headed," Al reminded me. "We'll have to carry enough for two days."

The plan was to stay on the mountain for two days and one night. Even though I was using a lot of lightweight, high-tech gear (extreme winter equipment, my rifle, and other hunting equipment), the water pushed both our packs well over fifty pounds.

We crossed the river in daylight and put on our climbing boots and crampons, winter traction devices that attach to your boots. We didn't bring Al's climbing ropes because we were already maxed out weight-wise. Our food consisted of a few sandwiches, protein, and granola bars.

Up the mountain we went.

It's one thing to climb straight up a mountain. It's another thing to do it with more than fifty pounds on your back. Because you never know if you're going to get stuck on a cliff or other terrain, that pack has to go wherever you go. It's your lifeline. Without it, you'll die.

Another huge obstacle that I initially didn't foresee was the effort it would take to get through the alders. In these extreme remote locations, the alders are unreal. Imagine thick, dense bushes twelve to fifteen feet tall. They form a prison around you. Branches overlap and go every direction. A patch of alder bushes can span a hundred feet without a break.

As we made our way up the vertical incline, we had to constantly push and pull our equipment, going around, under, and through the alders. And when I grabbed onto the alders for leverage, much of the time I ended up grabbing Devil's club or wild rose. Their little stickers went right through my gloves, and we ended up with hands filled with splinters again.

By the end of the first day, we made it up the rockslide and through the lower levels of the alders. At the base of the first set of cliffs, we got out our bivouacs and set up camp for the night. It was difficult to find enough flat ground for even one person to sleep.

The nights were long. It got dark around half past five in the evening, and the sun didn't come up until around seven in the morning.

Because it was so late in the year, we'd have over thirteen hours of darkness in our claustrophobic bivouacs. Once the sun went down, the temperature dropped from freezing cold to ridiculous cold. We couldn't build a fire because we didn't want to spook the goats.

The next morning, I went out to take a GPS reading before we started up the mountain. As I packed up, Al came racing toward me.

"Grab your spotting scope and rifle," he called. "I can see goats a couple hundred yards above our camp, including one good billy goat."

We started up the mountain to try to intercept where we thought the goats were heading. After a couple hours, we never saw them again, so we returned to camp.

Then we decided to move our camp up to the next elevation on the mountain, where we'd seen the most goats from our camp by the river. We loaded up and started a second level ascent.

This was going to be more dangerous. We had to work our way through the cliffs to get to the upper part of the mountain. Making matters worse, the cliffs were covered in a skiff of snow, just enough to gum up the spikes on our crampons.

"Don't fall," Al warned me. "That wouldn't look good for me, would it?"

"It probably wouldn't, but it'd be a whole lot worse for me!"

We began to work our way across the cliff faces. I was about to learn, yet again, the importance of focus and taking one step at a time. At one point, it didn't look like I could make it. I couldn't go back because of my position on the cliff. Below me was a drop of 100 to 200 feet. When I did look down, my imagination went wild, thinking the worst, so I learned not to look down.

That's when I learned an important lesson in hunting and in life: don't focus on all the bad things that might happen. Just tackle tough challenges one step at a time.

In this case, going forward and up were my only options. I couldn't go back or down.

As we moved across the cliff face, I tried to always have three secure points of contact to lessen the risk. One hand and two feet, or two hands and one foot. Three points had to be secure before I tested for my next hold and gave up my previous one. Any new hold that I grabbed onto might crumble. My foot might slip off the side. But because I could only look forward, I had to practice severe focus. In dicey situations like these, I learned I wouldn't survive if I thought ahead to where I wanted to end up, or if I lost concentration on those three points of contact. I was doing something risky, but in the safest way possible.

And that's what investing is like—calculated risk, as opposed to outright risk.

To keep from falling, every move I made had to be focused. Nothing could be hurried. Patience was paramount. I had to kick the snow off my crampon with each step. When I looked back, I could no longer see the path I took to get where I was. Once I was in the middle of it, I had to keep going.

After crossing the cliff faces, we continued up the mountain through more alders. We were able to find some goat trails to help speed our ascent. That was our best path—when we could actually find an animal-cut trail.

We made it to the top and could see goats on the peaks around us.

"There's a good billy goat." Al and I pointed out several record-book goats within shooting distance.

"I don't see any that we'd be able to get to after shooting them," I said eventually.

And that's the entire point.

It's not about shooting the first goat you see. It's about finding that trophy. We passed on all kinds of goats because we were looking for a record.

At one point, I saw a male goat start putting the moves on a female goat. She wanted nothing to do with him, though. Spurned, the male goat began head-butting her. Then he backed up, lowered his head, charged, and rammed the female goat. This male goat broke her shoulder; I could see it swinging loose, wrecked.

At another point, I spotted a golden eagle circling above a goat. Now, this goat had decided to climb a 350-foot-tall pinnacle, which is a narrow mountain peak that goes straight up and ends in a point at the top. For the life of me, I could not figure out how the goat got up there. It looked so bizarre—like a goat could defy the laws of physics. I couldn't help thinking, *Can goats fly?*

All of a sudden, the eagle dove at the goat, soaring down and past it. *Wow*, I thought. *That's pretty wild.*

The eagle continued to swoop around and past the goat.

Over the years, I've had a couple experiences with swooping eagles while out on cliffs. They have such large wingspans that they can block out the sun above you, creating huge shadows that make you startle and jerk your head up. It feels like being hunted, like this bird of prey is about to pick you up and carry you away.

This Golden Eagle dove down for a final time and hit that goat straight on, nailing his prey hard enough that it lost its balance and fell off the pinnacle. At the bottom of the 350-foot drop, the goat smashed into the rocks below—dead. Lunchtime for the eagle. It swooped down to land on the goat and began pulling its flesh apart.

So obviously, goats have evolved to live up in the mountains because very few predators can get them that high up. But they can't always escape the Golden Eagles above them.

And that's how an eagle can kill a goat.

➤━━━⊶⊷➤

Up this high, big boulders would also break off and roar down those vertical ravines into the gorges below. We could hear the rocks breaking and falling all the time. Even if we wanted to shoot one of the goats and retrieve it from where it fell below, we'd get smashed by falling rocks once we got down there.

So the challenge was more complicated than just locating a record-book goat. It had to be accessible visually *and* physically.

By the end of the second day, we were running out of food and water. The lack of food wasn't too much of a concern, but running out of water wasn't an option. I'd dealt with dehydration before. Its effects are a lot like hypothermia. A person experiencing dehydration becomes passive, delirious, and just wants to sleep. Getting someone off the mountain in that condition becomes impossible. Going down the mountain and bringing water back up to them would take too long.

Because it had taken so much effort to get up the mountain, we decided to stay another day and keep a close eye on each other in case we had to bail out if either of us started showing signs.

Around midnight, we set up our bivouacs on a trail with alders, the only flat ground we could find. Around midnight, I heard something nearby crossing through the brush. Bivouacs are like cocoons. They trap you inside them with warmth, but that also means they are very difficult to get out of—especially when your adrenaline spikes and you need to get out fast.

I could feel this animal breathing heavily behind my head. Because there was no way I'd be able to get out of the bivouac fast enough, I started pounding on the Gore-Tex material from inside, hoping to startle it. The animal took off, and I could hear several others go with it.

After the fun was over, I asked Al, "Did you see any of that?"

He was shaking his head. "I can't believe it."

Al had heard several goats walking toward his bivouac. He'd pulled out his pistol and took aim. "But I didn't want to shoot you in the back of the head."

"Thanks for that," I chuckled.

Instead, Al had sat up sharply, which caused the goats to run down the trail toward my bag.

"I swear, one of them lowered its head and started stamping its hooves," he said. "It was going to charge you."

That would have been lights out for me. Luckily, that was when I started hitting the back of my bivouac.

We lived to hunt another day.

On the third day, we were out of food, and our limited bottled water had frozen. At this point, the lack of water can start playing with your mind. Because you're so aware you need it, you tune into the sound of the rapids a few thousand feet below and start to obsess about it, like you're dying of thirst.

I found it ironic. The same water that was so dangerous when we navigated the canoe through it on the way up the river was the same water that we needed to stay alive.

We continued to look for the right goat in the right place, but it was beginning to seem impossible.

"We've got to bail out tomorrow." Al called it. I agreed.

The following morning, Al and I knew we were pushing our luck, but we were both unwilling to give up that first light. Climbing out of my bivouac on day four, I could see a goat sleeping on a ledge below us. I pulled my boots on and moved to take a look.

Once again, the goat was gone—almost as if there were white ghosts on the mountain with us. Time to bail off the mountain.

Eight painful hours later, we made it back down to camp and got some food. Greatest meal ever.

Time to head back down the river. We packed our gear into the canoe and started out. Because it was so late in the year, the river was slowly freezing from the banks inward. It got so shallow, with less and less running water, we had to start emptying gear from the canoe to get down the river.

When we made it back to the airboat, we discovered all its batteries had died.

We had no other option but to ditch the airboat. That meant we still had fifteen miles down rougher rapids to get through in only a canoe.

The sun was getting lower and lower, and we were pushing and pushing to get back to the trailhead where we'd left the truck and would head back to Haines. Out of nowhere, a massive Golden Eagle started riding the air currents above the river in front of us, doing this huge swoop back and forth, from one bank to the other. It stayed in front of us for several miles.

After so many days up the mountain, with so many challenges, it was like God himself was taking us out of there. At the end of yet another grueling trip, that image hit me. I'll never forget it.

As I sat on the plane flying home, I felt like I'd been run over by a truck. My hands were filled with splinters; my eyes were sunburned; and my back, knees, and right shoulder ached. I'd tried getting a record-book mountain goat in Alaska twice. It was time to take everything I'd learned into account, do some more research, give myself better options, and increase my odds so that on my third attempt, I'd succeed.

CHAPTER 8

EXPECT BEAR MARKETS; BE POSITIONED FOR BULL MARKETS

In Chapter 6, I introduced you to the third principle of true wealth, "Don't panic," and explored four ways that you can incorporate it into your life. "Don't panic" is all about how you react to moments in your life—when something goes wrong that you didn't expect, when you make a mistake, when there's no way to avoid the short and furious rapids that come at you, when you have a near-death experience.

The fourth principle of true wealth is "Expect bear markets; be positioned for bull markets," and it builds on the third principle. Both principles help you prepare for and get through difficult experiences, and even come out the other side happier and more successful than before. But the fourth principle tackles a different type of hardship and challenge: the longer periods of time that turn acute panic into chronic strain and prolonged pressure.

You'll notice in Chapter 7, the story about hunting mountain goat, that the time period I discussed is much longer than any other hunting story in this book. I took two trips to Alaska, twelve months apart, and on both attempts I didn't pull the trigger because none of the mountain goats I saw would make it into the top ten in the world. Both trips turned into hunting experiences that I characterize as an extreme, grueling grind. Often, they are longer than the average hunt—sometimes by choice, and other times because of external conditions. They also *feel* longer and more drawn-out, typically because conditions are more dangerous than usual. Not having the right mountain gear, running out of food and water, and risking dehydration all count as dangerous situations. For someone like me who commits to staying as long as necessary to get the job done, those long stretches stuck in the metaphorical (and sometimes real) trenches, waiting to get the win or for conditions to change, require a different type of mental strength and skill. That's what this chapter is all about.

What Are Bear and Bull Markets?

The first thing you need to know to understand the fourth principle of true wealth are some basics about bear and bull markets. "Bear market" and "bull market" are financial investment terms used to describe general trends in the stock market or economy. In a bear market, stock prices fall or are expected to fall, typically by at least 20 percent (and often more), over a sustained period of time—usually several months. Investor pessimism, fear, and a general lack of confidence in the economy are common in a bear market. As a result, investors often sell stocks in an effort to limit their losses, which further drives down stock prices.

In a bull market, stock prices rise or are expected to rise, typically by at least 20 percent (and often more), over a sustained period of time—usually several months or even years. Investor optimism, confidence, and a general expectation of future economic growth are common in a bull market. This leads to investors buying stocks to take advantage of the rising prices and potential for future gains, which further drives up stock prices.

Now, as a hunter, I can definitely appreciate these two terms. "Bear" and "bull" markets are thought to have originated from the way these animals attack their prey. A bear swipes its paws downward, while a bull thrusts its horns upward. This imagery reflects the direction of the stock market, with a bear market representing a downward trend and a bull market representing an upward trend. (Really, what else could I, a hunter *and* a financial advisor, have done to name this fourth principle any better?)

Perhaps most importantly, bear and bull markets follow each other in cycles over time. One comes after the other, comes after the other, comes after the other. Investors and financial advisors like me pay close attention to these trends and use them to make investment decisions and attempt to predict future market performance. This is what the investment strategies and models that I began creating over thirty-seven years ago are built on and do effectively.[1]

In the same way that many similarities can be drawn between big game hunting and financial investing, bear and bull markets can be used to describe and understand the cyclical nature of ups and downs that we all go through in life. In fact, I began to introduce this topic in Chapter 6 with my story about whitewater rafting in the Grand Canyon, and how understanding the nature of the river—sometimes it's smooth and peaceful, while other times it churns and moves like a rocket—can help us acknowledge that panic is inevitable if we don't prepare for it. The same applies for life's longer periods of struggle; if we don't prepare for them, they'll affect us more than they have to and even lead to chronic problems over time. But there's something else we also have to prepare and be positioned for.

Recognizing that life is naturally cyclical—and that we have to accept the cycles of life, instead of trying to change or avoid challenges and struggles—is essential to being able to hunt for true wealth and real happiness. If every time one of life's "downward trends" catches you off guard, and you feel hopeless, eventually you won't be able to find your footing again on the upswing. Your resilience will erode, your relationships will suffer, and the experiences that could have brought you happiness and success will pass you by. Remember: there's always going to be another down, followed by another up, followed by another down, and so on. While much of this chapter is about preparing

---

1 See Appendix A for disclosures.

yourself for the grueling grinds that come with life, your hunt for true wealth is equally dependent on your ability to internalize the fact that *another up is always coming!*

Too many people forget what the cycle of life means for them. It means you have to hang on and ride out the struggle. It means you have to make sure the difficult periods of life don't prevent you from enjoying the wonderful parts of life. And it means you have to expect bear markets, but *also* position yourself for bull markets.

In the rest of this chapter, I break down this fourth principle as it relates to finding success in both financial investing and that deeper, more gratifying experience of true wealth. First, I use the 2008 financial crisis and pandemic economic shock to explain why timing is critical and sorting fact from fiction is imperative during bear markets. Then, I bring together the toolbox of fundamentals that you need to learn and practice to survive a bear market, many of which I've introduced and built on throughout this book already—because they're just that important. And I share more hunting stories for you to enjoy and learn from.

Riding the Roller Coaster of Financial Investing

When you see your accounts go down 20, 40, 50 percent, what are you going to do? Importantly, it's not *if* you see your accounts go down. It's *when* you see them go down.

I've been through a number of financial bear markets: in 1987, 1998, 2000, 2008, and 2020. The 1987 bear market is when I proved to myself and others that the investment strategies and models I'd been creating were the real deal. If ever I needed convincing that I'm at my best when I embrace challenges, that bear market did it for me. We all need trials by fire, and some of the greatest success we experience in life can come right after bear markets.[2]

The 2008 Financial Crisis: Timing Is Critical

The 2008 financial crisis—which actually spanned from August 2007 to March 2009—was not a normal bear market. It would be

---

2 See Appendix A for disclosures.

better described as a financial collapse, where everything went down except for Treasury bonds. But even a collapse doesn't mean you run for the hills. We were very active at Paragon during this time. By April 2008, the markets had dropped about 25 percent, and I knew it hadn't finished yet. In October 2008, President Bush signed the Troubled Asset Relief Program (TARP) into law, authorizing the government to buy up to $700 billion in troubled assets to stabilize the financial system. At the same time, the US stock market experienced its largest one-day point drop in history, with the Dow Jones Industrial Average falling 777.68 points.

Every time incoming President Obama (who would be sworn in on January 20, 2009) went on television, the market would drop significantly. We watched for those types of patterns. By the end of October, the "bottom watch indicators" that we track—five to six metrics that indicate when the market has reached whatever bottom it's going to reach—were screaming at us to buy. (The best time to buy is when the market is at its lowest, right before it goes up again. The trick is accurately defining when it reaches that low.) Now, at this point, everything was down 40 percent, which meant I'd get anything I bought *40 percent cheaper* than where it had been. However, I wasn't fully convinced we'd reached the very bottom of the market, despite those bottom watch indicators, because this was no ordinary bear market.

Despite knowing the market may not have bottomed out yet, I started buying anyway. Why would I do that? Well, most people would be worried it wasn't done dropping, and they would fixate on those losses. But I was looking three years out. Buying at 40 percent cheaper is fantastic, and if I held my positions for three years, I was confident I'd likely make a lot of money on them, even if the market continued to go down 10, 20, 30 percent more in the interim. I was building a core position to hold past the short-term market lows.

From October 2008 to March 2009, the market did lose another 25 percent, which sucked. In the big picture, though, it didn't matter. The true bottom came in March 2009. From then on, we had a huge rally back to the upside. Everything I'd been buying started doing really well, really fast, so we capitalized on this "Merry Christmas" opportunity.

When the stars align like this, you can supercharge your wealth. But getting "Merry Christmas" returns like this isn't a long-term strategy. Over the long haul, the market will trend up or down, so you should practice all the fundamentals of investing right. Along the way, though, and whenever you get a chance, capitalize on "Merry Christmas" moments. Just don't count on them as a long-term strategy.[3]

Many of the investors who got destroyed during this bear market were people who came in around 2005, during the middle of the bull market that came before (from 2003 to 2007), and weren't able to adapt to the extremes that came after. They went all in during the bull market, sat back, and when the markets tanked 40 percent, they were suddenly convinced that this was the worst thing they'd ever done in their life. So they bailed out at a 40-percent loss—right before the market turned in March 2009. And because they were so emotionally wrecked from the drop, they became convinced it would be impossible to know when the market was going to turn around. This lack of resilience prevented them from jumping back in, so they weren't able to capitalize on the real opportunities of the market recovery.

The 2008 financial crisis was a devastating bear market, which meant for a prolonged period of time it felt like no one wanted to invest. But that's precisely when you do need to invest—strategically. The timing is critical. You also have to be looking beyond the short-term losses. Ultimately, the smart investors stayed with the market's roller-coaster drop and rode it back up to the new highs.[4]

COVID-19: Media Fiction and Real Facts

The coronavirus pandemic closed down the economy in a way we had never seen before. Before March 2020, like most of the world, I had never heard the word "COVID-19" or "coronavirus." Then, suddenly, it was everywhere—a microscopic, viral agent that destroyed nearly $15 trillion in global stock market wealth in just over a month.

---

3 See Appendix A for disclosures.

4 See Appendix A for disclosures.

In almost thirty-five years of investing and managing through some of the worst bear markets in history, I had never seen anything like it.

Bear markets are usually caused by basic financial conditions and expectations becoming extreme and out of sync. This bear market was caused by a tiny virus—but also extreme media hype and distortions. Almost every media source that I follow proclaimed it was the end of the world. Some even went so far as to guarantee we were witnessing the start of another Depression, perhaps even equal to 1929. This led to uncertainty, followed by extreme fear, and finally panic.

Inaccurate information can destroy you when it comes to investing. Media forecasts usually do more harm than good. During the March 2020 meltdown, every single person I saw on mainstream media claimed, almost with religious fervor, that this would *not* be a V-shaped recovery. As you either know or suspect, a V-shaped recovery is characterized by a sharp decline in economic activity, followed by a rapid and robust rebound. The decline is typically caused by a specific shock or event, but once the shock is addressed, economic activity can quickly bounce back as consumers, businesses, and investors regain confidence and begin to spend and invest again.

In retrospect, media predictions were completely wrong, and investors who believed their predictions and followed their advice lost a lot of money. The amazing thing is that those pundits and forecasters are all still working away at the same news desks. They're still full of advice. They still have zero accountability. They do this year after year, through every up and down, and people continue to listen to them.

To invest successfully, you have to sift through fact and fiction, and be able to identify both correctly. You have to invest based on reality. This is what our quantitative models are designed to do at Paragon, eliminating much of the noise and opinion guesswork and distilling the market down to the numbers that show what's actually happening. Then we follow those numbers.[5]

Contrary to what the media proclaimed, the major market indexes reversed course right after their initial thirty-day plunge. On the year,

5 See Appendix A for disclosures.

the Dow Industrials gained 9.6 percent, and the S&P 500 was up 18.4 percent. What had been the "end of the world" turned out just fine. I never heard any retractions from the talking heads in the media.

At Paragon, our greatest returns have often come after market downturns. Data from Linsco Private Ledger (LPL) Research show that bull markets often have strong returns in the first recovery year when they follow a decline of at least 30 percent.[6] The rally that followed 2020's bear market, which reached a 34-percent decline, was no exception. The average increase in the first year of the six bull markets that have occurred since World War II and followed a 30 percent or greater decline is 41 percent. That's an impressive one-year return and a clear demonstration that bear markets usually end unexpectedly. Investors who run from the market or move to cash for safety during the decline frequently find themselves missing out. And, indeed, the first-year return of 75 percent after 2020's bottom ranks as the highest ever, exceeding 2009's second place return of 69 percent.

On average, all the bull markets in question have been positive in year two as well, with an average return for the S&P 500 of 17 percent. However, the second year is usually quite volatile, with an average pullback (a decline within an upward trend) of 10 percent. So, what helps drive returns? Momentum, an expanding economy, higher corporate profits, and a generally accommodative policy from the Federal Reserve. With what you now know about how bear and bull markets work, though, the more useful question to ask is: How do you build wealth over time?

To build wealth, you have to invest in things that go up faster than other alternatives. The downside is that what goes up faster over time also occasionally goes down faster. As you've seen in this discussion, the most difficult part of the program is that sometimes your investments stay down for a while. And the greatest stress comes from never knowing exactly where in the cycle we are until after the fact.

---

6 Ryan Detrick, "Six Things to Know about Bear Markets," *LPL Research*, May 18, 2022, https://lplresearch.com/2022/05/18/six-things-to-know-about-bear-markets/, accessed July 21, 2023.

But we do know that we are in a cycle.

At the beginning of this chapter, I explained that investor optimism is common during bull markets but not during bear markets. One important secret to succeeding in financial investing—and the hunt for true wealth more broadly—is to use the fact that we are always in a cycle. That fact can help you retain your optimism through the bear markets and hard times. If you can do this, you'll be so far ahead of most other people. As I said in the introduction to this book, true wealth is rooted in optimism. Pessimism is the true enemy of progress, success, and happiness. So many people today say it won't work, it can't happen, this isn't possible. It is. Just make it happen—by staying optimistic.

Optimism is one of the thirteen values of true wealth. Now, let's touch on three more. First, to navigate market cycles, you have to practice real honesty with yourself. You have to be honest about what your risk tolerance is. If you get it wrong and bite off more than you can chew, you'll bail out of the market at exactly the wrong time. You have to be honest about how emotionally invested you are at any given time, actively working on your self-awareness and self-control so that you don't make decisions that you'll come to regret.

Second, you have to live in alignment with yourself. As you'll remember, bear markets are usually caused when financial conditions and expectations get extreme and out of sync. These periods can easily pull you out of sync too. Don't let them. Stay true to yourself, maintain your equilibrium and personal center of gravity, and make sure your beliefs and values match how you're living your life. Living in alignment will help you avoid getting emotionally wrecked on the roller coaster of bear and bull markets.

Third, I strongly encourage you to take up a mantra I've carried with me my entire life: "I was born ready." When someone asks you (or you ask yourself), "Are you ready?" Your response should always be, "I was born ready." Welcome whatever the world has to throw at you. Don't shrink from the bad. Don't diminish yourself or anything that makes up part of your life. Live every day like you were born ready, and you will find the empowerment you need to ride the roller coaster, hunting for true wealth and the success that you deserve.

Hunting Antelope in the Book Cliffs of Utah

In 1993, I drew an antelope tag in the Book Cliffs of Utah. Before then, I'd only hunted deer in the area, but my friend Rich Lowe knew the antelope hunting situation well. So he and I made a couple trips out to scope and scout the area on our four-wheelers, looking for antelope that we could hunt with a compound bow.

The Book Cliffs—named because they resemble a shelf of books—are a range of remote desert plateaus and canyons on the border between Utah and Colorado. Quakies and pines fill the canyons, and mountain-fed streams carve through many of them. Soon after we arrived, Rich and I found a watering spot that we thought antelope would be attracted to and dug a three- to four-foot hole beside it. Then we covered it with brush to create a blind that would be invisible to animals.

On the evening before the day of the official hunt, we returned to the Book Cliffs and set up camp, very excited for the coming hunt. The next morning, we hiked to the watering spot and the blind we had dug out—only to discover someone had put something in the water that turned it a strange color and odor. We knew animals would be avoiding it as a result. All that preparation we'd done had been flushed down the toilet.

Then we hiked back to camp where I'd parked my white Chevy Blazer and made our second discovery of the day—a flat tire. We were sixty miles from the nearest *anything*, and it was a rough dirt road all the way out in the middle of nowhere.

What an ordeal. First, Rich and I changed the tire using my spare. Next, we packed everything up and headed to Vernal, Utah, to find a shop that could patch the tire. Once we took care of that, we headed back to the Book Cliffs but had to spend more time making sure we got back to the legal hunting area instead of the adjacent Indian reservation. (GPS devices had not yet become common use.) That ate up even more of our day.

Finally, we were back in business. But the day had disappeared. Zero hunting accomplished. We camped out that night and got up the following morning ready to hunt. For most of the day, we didn't see any good antelope.

Then, near sundown, I spotted a phenomenal antelope. He was huge. Strangely enough, his horns looked even bigger than most trophy antelope because he had a comparatively smaller body.

With bow hunting, you usually only get one shot. If I missed, by the time I notched another arrow, the antelope would be long gone.

I crawled through the sagebrush, getting closer and closer. Forty-four feet out from the antelope, I stopped, pushed into a kneeling position, and began to draw back my seventy-pound bow. Ready and waiting, all I needed him to do was bend over and start feeding. A distracted antelope would be much less inclined to sense any danger coming his way.

The antelope wouldn't start feeding, though, and my arm was getting wasted holding back the bow. The longer I waited, the more likely the antelope would become aware of me. Finally, I decided that since I had a broadside shot, I'd let my arrow fly.

As soon as I let go, the antelope heard the string and spooked. He jumped forward, high and powerful, then took off. My arrow flew right through the spot where he'd been standing. I could practically see the animal's outline of where he'd just been!

This miss was a major bummer. Up to that point, he was the biggest antelope I'd seen in the Book Cliffs. Rich and I had already taken a couple trips out to the Cliffs to get everything set up. All our energy from the time, effort, and preparation that came before this shot got compressed into the space of thirty seconds; I could *taste* this shot. That's why it really sucked when the arrow missed its mark.

Rich and I camped another night.

The next morning, we woke up and found ourselves really feeling our bad experience up to this point. It felt like ages had passed since our enthusiasm at the watering spot. Since then, it had been disappointment after unexpected obstacle after frustrating near miss. But Rich and I got back to it—scouting and glassing all over. Eventually, I caught sight of the same antelope as yesterday. He had meandered to about a mile away, grazing alongside a ravine. We closed the distance to about 300 yards. Then I got down on the ground and began crawling through the sagebrush.

There we were, the antelope and I, together again, only forty yards separating us for a second time.

Within seconds, I had to make a decision about where to aim my bow. I could do the exact same thing I'd done yesterday and hope the antelope didn't hear the string this time, or I could aim slightly in front of the antelope, guessing that if he jumped again, that's the direction he'd go.

I chose the second option and led the antelope about three feet.

I let go.

The antelope jumped right where I'd calculated he would jump. My arrow hit him perfectly behind the shoulder through the lungs. He took off running straight down the ravine on pure adrenaline. We found him about a hundred yards away.

At the time, this trophy animal ended up taking number two in the state of Utah with a bow—an amazing outcome for a real trial of a hunt that teaches two important life lessons about bear markets.

First, don't give up. Even when multiple bad experiences pepper your challenge, turning it into a tribulation that feels interminable and would be easy to quit, keep going. On this hunt, despite the bad experiences leading up to the second successful shot, I *never* considered saying *screw it* and going home. Quitting is just not how I think. Once I'd seen this phenomenal animal (my goal), I knew I had to stay out for as long as it took. Use the *possibility* of your achievement, even if it's not guaranteed, to spur you on.

Second, when you strategize, plan, and try to accomplish something, don't only or always go right toward your target. Consider aiming in front of the target. Go to where you think the opportunity will be, instead of where you can see it is now. Likewise, in investing, we trust our data-based models to inform us as we buy stocks in anticipation of where we think they're going, not where they are right now. Always plan to go where the stock is headed. This is exactly what I did during the 2008 financial crisis when I looked three years out, instead of focusing on the short-term losses, and got awesome returns as a result.[7]

Similarly, in life it's a mistake to focus only on where things are right now for you and forget about envisioning where they might be later. As hockey great Wayne Gretzky famously said of his success, "Skate to where the puck is going to be, not where it has been."

Learn and Practice the Fundamentals

I was speaking with my daughter Katie recently. She donates thirty hours a week of her time to lead the Live Your Dream Foundation, which we founded as a family in 2010. The foundation gives scholarships to single mothers who want to pursue higher education and better provide for their children.

In 2022, we set a goal to raise $150,000 for the foundation. For ten months, Katie struggled to make any sort of dent in that goal. Funders bailed and dropped out left, right, and center. None of her pitches converted. Every month, the goal seemed to draw further and further away. That's the essence of a bear market in the context of fundraising for a charitable organization.

But Katie kept chugging along. She networked. She went out and made her pitches over and over. She drew on her eight years of experience leading the foundation.

"It's unreal," she told me, full of enthusiasm, when we spoke. "In the last six weeks, we've had $60,000 in gifts come in that we didn't even know were coming."

Over the course of the year, Katie did what she had to do—and she kept doing it. She didn't falter. She didn't call it quits or make any drastic changes to her fundraising methods. And one day, things started to come together. If she hadn't kept going, and going, and going, that wouldn't have happened.

This conversation with Katie helped me crystallize a central moral of my hunting stories and overarching lesson for life and finance that I want readers to take away from this book: don't stop, even when you

---

7 See Appendix A for disclosures.

can't see the finish line. Keep chugging along. Have patience and com-mitment. At times, you won't feel like you're making progress. You won't see any tangible progress. You may start to doubt that anything will ever change for the better.

To get through these long periods in between successes, you have to learn and execute on the fundamentals. You have to keep doing what you have to do. You won't know when it will all come together—or if it will come together at all. But you do know that if you stop, it won't come together. So the only real option you have is to keep going.

Patience. Perseverance. Commitment. Consistency. Hard work. These are the fundamental *qualities of character* that you have to bring to bear during bear markets. I do my best to practice them during every hunt I go on. They're also what has gotten me through some of the toughest bear markets of my personal life: the death of my son-in-law, the fallout from my son's addiction to gambling, the fights I've had to take on over frivolous lawsuits, and the most extreme bear markets in my lifetime with the market going down 50 percent.

You also have to learn and practice the fundamental *strategies and processes* that will see you succeed in hunting, investing, and life. Throughout this book, I've been giving you a toolbox of these strategies and processes. Let's bring them all together so far:

1. Follow the seven steps to building financial wealth.

2. Do your research and due diligence.

3. Identify and work with excellent guides and advisors.

4. Invest in quality gear, tools, and resources that will serve you over the long haul.

5. Build your knowledge, experience, and skills over time.

6. Set and reset your risk tolerance properly.

7. Increase your odds and keep your options open.

8. Pivot when necessary.

Being mentally disciplined is essential, but if you're disciplined while practicing the wrong strategies and processes, you'll never get where you want to go. You won't succeed unless you're both disciplined and following the right strategy.

If you go to my trophy room in the downstairs of my home, the average time it's taken me to kill any of those animals is about nine days. This is well past the time that most hunters stick around or even stay focused.

Most people start a hunt very committed to getting a really good animal. The first and second day, oh, let me tell you, they're so pumped and so committed. They get up early, and their focus is exemplary. They're paying attention to what it means to be a good hunter. Then, on day three, they're going to shoot anything they can freakin' find. That's the path they take because climbing mountains and wading across rivers and navigating through back country is hard. They fizzle out, a switch flips, and they'll shoot anything. But to get the real trophy animals, you have to stay focused; you have to be extremely patient; and you have to put in the work to *do it right*. Leopard hunting, for example, is probably 90 percent boredom and 10 percent the highest adrenaline rush you've ever experienced in your entire life.

Another way to think of this is that you have to put in the time. You have to become one with the animals. You have to be out there with them. It's by practicing the fundamentals that you come to have full trust in your training, just like Katie trusted her training and experience. Let me tell you another hunting story that shows exactly what the difference is between hunting done right and hunting done wrong.

My third hunting trip to the Book Cliffs of Utah took place during muzzleloader season. This meant hunters couldn't use rifles or bows in the area. At that time, traditional muzzleloaders had good accuracy up to about 150 yards. The farther away you get from your target, the less power and accuracy a muzzleloader has. When you shoot an animal with a muzzleloader, you shouldn't approach it too quickly because it can take some time for it to bleed out. If it's wounded but still alive when you get to it, the animal may jump up and attack you, or it may take off faster than it would if it hadn't seen you. Even animals that are bleeding out can escape you.

So, there I was in the Book Cliffs, lying on the ground in my ghillie suit, well camouflaged into the shrub-and-grass terrain. I'd been glassing a good-looking buck for a solid hour. I was locked onto it fully and perfectly—the type of connection all true hunters chase. Then, suddenly, the quiet broke when four men started shooting over the hill behind me at the deer; it went down instantly.

That pissed me off. I'd been stalking this deer for a day and a half, and these bozos just stumbled across it. Not to mention I could've been caught in the crossfire! They celebrated like yahoos and ran down to the deer. Before they reached it, though, the deer jumped up, whirled around, and took off.

The men were upset, distraught, and confused. They couldn't figure out how the deer had survived when they'd clearly hit it. Instead of following its trail, these sloppy hunters shrugged, went back to their truck, and had another beer.

I found the deer's trail and spent another two days tracking it. At dusk, I finally got a profile on it and took a shot that I had full confidence in. Because darkness had almost fallen, I didn't have enough daylight left to approach the deer. I went back to camp, passed the night, and came back the next morning to locate the animal. After some patient searching, I found a blood trail and followed it. When I caught up to the deer later that morning, I found it dead.

The deer had a bullet hole right through one of its antlers. Whichever sloppy hunter had hit it, their shot had only stunned the animal. After everyone else had called it quits, I stayed on that deer and focused on the fundamentals—both qualities of character and proper hunting strategies and practices. That's why I have a one-of-a-kind set of antlers, with a perfect bullet hole right through it, mounted on my wall.

When you learn and practice your fundamentals, you are better able to withstand bear markets while also being positioned for bull markets. Never forget that another bull market will come. Those fundamentals will serve you through the entire, unending cycle. Really, once you master them, you're well on your way to true wealth.

In the next chapter, I continue the saga of trying to get a trophy mountain goat in Alaska. Even after two unsuccessful attempts, I wasn't done yet. Giving up wasn't an option. I tried again, practicing my fundamentals: I did more research; I found another exceptional guide; I made sure I had all the right gear; and I pivoted in a way that would increase my odds. And, of course, I had another extraordinary, hair-raising, jaw-dropping experience.

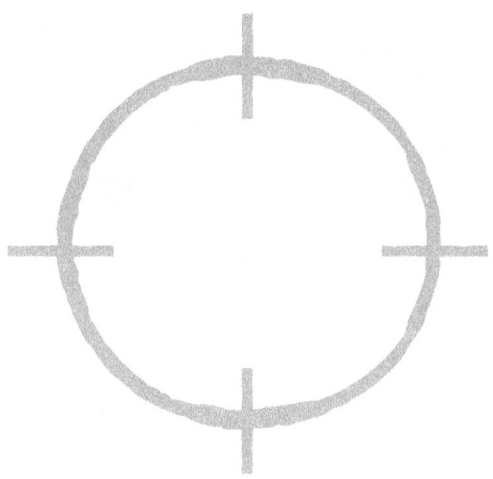

CHAPTER 9

HUNTING MOUNTAIN GOAT IN BRITISH COLUMBIA, THE THIRD ATTEMPT

I n early October 2006, I decided to chase a record-book goat for the third time.

I needed to pivot, though. If something's not working, you pivot. The timing of a pivot has to be right, but the conditions and resources have to be right too. Sometimes you might be walking away from a great opportunity, but you have to play the odds. I'd already hunted twice in the area of Alaska that had the biggest goats, but I hadn't seen anything I thought would make the Top 10 in the record books. Those two trips had been pretty grueling, and that location should have produced a top-tier goat, but it didn't. There's a time to focus on the fundamentals of big game trophy hunting—patience, focus, and doing things no one else does—but you've also got to recognize when to change course. Following the fundamentals is critical, but it won't do you any good if you're on the wrong track.

This time, instead of going to Alaska, I flew to Northern British Columbia, next to the Yukon border. Before finding this location, I'd done a ton of research. I knew I wanted to hunt an area where 1)

Rocky Mountain goats with record-book quality genetics lived with 2) enough remoteness, away from hunters and predators, for an animal to grow gigantic.

I'd heard about this specific hunting area up in British Columbia that had been closed for several years. About seven years prior, a hunting party had actually been up there hunting mountain goats, and at least one of the hunters had fallen from a cliff and died. The government shut the area down for a while. When I found out the area was being reopened, and I could be the first hunter back in there, my gut told me I had my pivot.

Reaching out to several guides, I eventually connected with a woman named Heidi Gutfrucht. She came recommended by the owner of *Huntin' Fool*, a newsletter at the time that later became a magazine. He called Heidi "tough as nails."

Now, I'd never encountered a woman outfitter before, and I'd never put a hunt (or my life) in a woman's hands before. But I knew that trekking into this rough, gnarly backcountry, she had to be tough.

It turned out, Heidi *was* a badass. In her midthirties to midforties, she had shoulder-length brown hair and strong, muscular legs capable of climbing anything. Solid, strong, and sure-footed, she couldn't be knocked over.

Heidi lived in Alberta, near an Indian reserve (Canadians' term for a "reservation"). One day, I heard, she got into it with a couple Indigenous guys. They'd been harassing her and had stolen her four-wheeler. When the police and justice system failed to help her, Heidi went over to their place on the reserve and lit their truck on fire, blowing it up!

So Heidi could hold her own.

Now, I did "forget" to tell my wife that a woman would be my guide on this hunt. Cathy trusts me completely (and I her), and we'd been happily married for twenty-five years by this point. I just didn't think it was necessary to add that complication to her mind, especially when I knew it would never turn into anything. I pick my battles. And very rarely does Cathy care to know the details of my hunts.

In general, when someone asks her, "Where's your husband?" my wife will shrug and say, "Oh, he went hunting."

"Well, where'd he go?"

Another shrug. "The mountains? Mongolia? Maybe Alaska."

Cathy trusts me—and can't be bothered with my hunting. It works perfectly for us. To this day, I'm not sure I ever even told my wife that Heidi guided me on that hunt.

For this hunt, I also had another complication. Over the years, I'd blown out my knee four times, mostly playing basketball. In my twenties, I tore the cartilage and ended up getting it fixed by a doctor who'd been run out of his previous job and town for being an idiot. I was young and stupid, though, and didn't do my research to find the right doctor.

After that first surgery, my knee didn't regain full stability. I kept playing basketball anyway. A year later, I blew it out again—worse this time. I tore my ACL, MCL, and PCL, the three ligaments that hold your entire knee together. That took quite a while to put back together and heal up. This time, I went to a legitimate doctor, and he did the surgery right.

In the years that followed, I blew out just the ACL twice more. Basketball, it turned out, took more of a toll on my knees than hunting ever did.

A couple months after blowing out my knee for the third time, I had two hunts planned. I also discovered that you can stabilize your leg with a brace, and it will still work, allowing me the mobility I needed. People will tell you that you can't go hunting with a blown-out knee. I say do whatever works for you. Just do your research first.

After those two hunts, I went to the surgeon and had the ACL replaced. I had a fourth surgery, also on my ACL, during the spring of 2006, before the fall when this mountain goat hunt took place. This wasn't going to be a normal hunt. I wouldn't just be hiking up a mountain. I knew the cliffs would be treacherous and the verticals extreme. I had to be able to move my legs properly.

Still healing from the spring surgery, I met with my doctor in October.

"As long as you have no deep-knee action, you should be okay," he told me. "No lunges or squat motions."

Well, crap, I thought. Squat motions make up a lot of a steep mountain climb.

"Screw it," I said to myself as I left the doctor's office. "I'm going to be the first person up in that reopened hunting area. I want that record goat."

The extra level of challenge—getting a goat with an injured knee—would make the accomplishment that much sweeter.

I'd gone to Alaska twice in November because I wanted to give the mountain goats time to develop their winter pelts. Most hunters go in September because the weather is much less extreme. But I wanted to get an *amazing* goat. Going hunting after knee surgery and going that late in the hunting season are comparable in terms of added challenge. Both made the hunt tougher. Both would make the win more spectacular.

Likewise, to become a successful investor, you usually have to go a different direction from everyone else. Sometimes you get in sync and ride the same wave as other investors—that's a good foundation to build confidence. But to achieve actual serious wealth, you also have to chase the extremes. You have to do the opposite of what everyone else is doing, while basing your decisions and moves on solid research and financial models you can depend on.

If everything is sold off and everything's gone to hell, nobody wants to invest. Well, that's when you've got to go in and invest. A rational person would say, "Markets are down 30 percent, why would I put my money in *that*? That sucks."

Because everyone looks at where you've been, they don't often look at where you're going. They extrapolate that wherever you've been will continue forever. It won't. Hunting areas run dry. You have to constantly be looking for new hunting areas and stacking the conditions in your favor—even when those conditions add to the challenge.

Similarly, when you invest in extremes, you're staring into the jaws of death—and you're okay with it because you believe that it's the right place to be. It's totally counterintuitive. As an investor, after you go to hell and back, though, the boost to your confidence is far greater than the confidence you gain from always going along with everyone else. With experience and investment success, I've learned how to overcome that type of extreme challenge. That experience has become indispensable.

When I first started investing, I had a lot less money. Back then, I had to put pretty much everything on the line. Most people in that situation are less likely to take the same risks I took. But that's how I live my life in everything I do. And that allowed me to gain the level of experience that I bring with me into every investment today. I took that same mentality with me into my third hunt for a record mountain goat.

I flew from Salt Lake City to Vancouver to Smithers, a little town up in Northern British Columbia. Then I went to Dease Lake, and from there on to Telegraph Creek. Those are both very small communities—too small to be considered towns. Another guide named John, whom Heidi employed as part of her main business hunting stone sheep (big rams), came with us as a packer to help bring all the meat out.

In Telegraph, I packed up all my gear and headed out to the base camp with Heidi and John. That's where we spent the first day, which had a phenomenal view. The camp was absolutely beautiful, by a high mountain lake and surrounded by cliffs and bluffs. Big, big country. It's the kind of place that when you set eyes on it, you know that hardly anyone in the world has seen that same sight. Gorgeous.

It's mind-blowing to me to think that we're all crammed in these cities, effectively living in boxes, when phenomenally beautiful places like this exist.

The previous two times I'd gone mountain goat hunting, our base camp had been next to a river at the bottom of a mountain, and we had to climb straight up its front side. This time, rather than going straight up the front, we approached the backside of a mountain by river, allowing us to hike up a more gradual 4,000-foot incline.

"It's like a stroll in the park," I laughed with Heidi.

John, Heidi, and I set out early in the morning and didn't reach the mountain top until late evening, after the sun had already set. The path we hiked up only had one clear trail. We came up on top and paused to look out over the cliffs—breathtaking. Then we set up camp. My knee was sore, but I took anti-inflammatories and painkillers throughout the trip to keep it mellowed out. I don't usually use trekking poles, but this time I did to offset the pain from the lingering instability in my knee.

On day two, we hiked the area extensively looking for goats. The basin that spread out below us was gigantic. Sheer cliffs covered both sides, and a river sat at the bottom that couldn't be accessed by boat. Its steep waterfalls and rough rapids made it too treacherous. In this part of the world, the farther you go back in and away from civilization, the bigger and more spectacular everything gets—and also more dangerous.

Glassing the cliffs around us, I had 10-power and 15-power binoculars, a 65-power spotting scope that I could dial in, my 300 ultra mag rifle, and all the other gear we needed. All total, our backpacks weighed around fifty pounds each. We saw quite a few goats, but all on the other side of the basin. The goats often got themselves into these ridiculous places, up the middle of 1,000-foot cliffs that went straight up and down.

Can these goats frickin' fly? I wondered as I had many times before. *How the crap do they get in these impossible places?*

The problem, then, became how we would physically access any goat we might shoot. We kept at it, though, hiking goat trails that went right along the sheer cliff tops. The drop-off on one side could be up to 2,500 feet and the other side anywhere between 200 and 1,000 feet, depending on the location. Walking along these narrow ridges with my gear, trekking poles, and a jacked-up knee required an extreme amount of focus and calm.

Goats live up in these places because of predators. Their horns and hooves aren't great for defending and protecting against wolves, so they've evolved to survive in these cliffs away from predators—except the occasional Golden Eagle. I remembered seeing that Golden Eagle fly along the ridge line and knock the big billy goat to his death 350 feet below, then follow it down to tear the goat apart and feast.

At one point, we spotted three goats on a ridge below us, heading straight toward us as they fed along the trail. We froze and watched; they didn't sense us. One turned out to be a nanny, and the two others were young billy goats—not what we were looking for. They passed right below us and never noticed us.

Further down the cliffs, we spotted a six-year-old billy goat.

"We can take him as our backup in case we don't find a record book," Heidi suggested. Male goats hit their prime between six to eight years, so he would have been a good trophy on most hunts.

"Nah," I decided. "We're only shooting a record-book goat."

We covered a lot of country and saw a few more goats on our side of the basin, but nothing special. Toward the end of the day, we located five more goats in the distance. They looked to be mature goats, likely billy goats based on the boxy sturdiness of their sides and the absence of kids in their group. One of them had separated himself from the other four; he had very dirty fur. Definitely the king of the group.

We were too far away to pinpoint his exact size, though, and darkness was falling. Our plan was to head back to the same bluff the following morning. After getting back to camp soaked from sweat and rain, we took off all our layers and laid them out to dry in the wind. Despite the late time of year and the six to twelve inches of snow on the ground, it rained quite a bit. The air held a lot of humidity.

"This is pointless," Heidi said. "Nothing ever dries out here unless we build a fire."

But we couldn't build a fire while hunting; any goats around us would spook.

We fixed our dinner of dehydrated, packaged food, heating it up in a cup on the teeny camping stove that we used to boil water. At that altitude, water takes longer to boil. After dinner, I took some more pills for the pain in my knee and went to bed.

On the third day, we headed back to where we'd seen those big solitary goats. We located three of them, sneaking up to watch them from about 1,000 yards away—about ten football fields, and that's relatively close. Closer now, we could see that one hadn't reached adulthood yet, and one only had a single horn from a fall. The third was bigger than the other two, but it wasn't the king we'd seen yesterday.

We watched them for about half an hour, when all of a sudden, they picked up our presence, stood up, and took off. On the next ridge over, about 300 yards away, we spotted a huge, dirty goat when he abruptly started running away from us. Even that brief glimpse told us he might be a shooter.

"He must've seen us," I said.

Then I realized he'd seen us first, before the other three goats, and before we'd seen him. When he spooked and ran, the other three goats followed suit. They moved into an area on the cliff faces that we couldn't see because of the steep angle.

Heidi gave me a "we're screwed" look and just said, "Damn." The huge billy had spooked so badly, we figured he'd likely stay in the cliffs for a long time. No choice but to move on.

"It looks like you're going to stay longer than planned," Heidi said. "We need to pack up and move to a new canyon."

She was as committed as me, and very excited to go after a record book because so few people put in what it takes to do it. Getting a Top 10 was a point of pride for her.

Heidi had never come so far into this area, but we decided to continue moving away from camp with the hope that we might get lucky and see something else. As we headed down the canyon, along the tops of the cliffs, Heidi picked up the track of the king that had spooked.

My excitement spiked. "Now *that* is a monster goat track."

We followed the track quite a while and eyeballed a goat below us. Not the king. We kept going, until the track went over the side of a ridge and disappeared. Goats could follow it, but we definitely couldn't. Glassing the area below, we tried to pick up the king again.

As we kept moving down the canyon, we caught sight of a patch of white about 100 yards off the top and about 240 yards from us on an angle. That patch of white wouldn't register to most people. But we got out our spotting scope and dialed in on it. It was fur.

We thought it might be our king but couldn't tell for sure. Just in case, we set up our tripod out of sight, and I got my gun on a dead rest. I checked the distance and angle: 232 yards and 32 degrees. Based on those measurements, I knew I had to set up for a 200-yard shot. The geometry of the shot was very important.

I waited. If the goat had bedded down over there, we could get stuck in one place and waste the rest of the day. It might have been the monster goat, but it might not. We didn't know, and we'd have to make a judgment call at some point. Should we stay or should we go?

We got lucky. After half an hour, the goat got up, changed position, and bedded again. For the first time, we could see it was him—the goat we were after.

The new angle I had on it allowed me to see its vitals. I shot.

The goat dropped, still. I'd hit it perfectly behind the shoulder, taking out its lungs. That's an almost instant death.

It doesn't get any better than this, I thought as Heidi, John, and I celebrated. Whooping, high fives, an outpouring of emotion.

Getting to the goat would be complicated, but he seemed pretty stable where he'd fallen on the ridge. It didn't look like he was going to roll over the side of the cliff—until he did.

We couldn't believe it.

"All right," I said, hoping he wouldn't fall far. "Fifty feet," I yelled. "Then he'll get stuck in the cliffs."

He didn't get stuck. He picked up speed, rolling over each ridge, dropping down to each landing below it. Picture a cartoon animal bouncing down the side of a mountain.

"A thousand feet," I said, disgusted, "and still going." *Holy shiz!* I thought to myself. *This isn't possible.*

Heidi started yelling too. "Not the river! Please, not the river!"

This was the ultimate "Oh, shiz" moment. We'd shot this amazing goat, and we couldn't do a thing to stop his tumble. If he hit the water at the bottom, the river would wash him away. We'd never find him.

Finally, the goat slammed into a huge boulder next to the river and stopped. Relief flooded us, and we celebrated again because at least we could still see where he had landed.

I turned to Heidi and said, "Let's move our camp back to the trail-head, get a boat, and go retrieve the goat."

"Good idea, except those rapids make the river impassable," she said. "We've got to go down through 1,800 feet of cliffs. Then we've got to haul him all the way back up."

That nice, happy hike up the backside of the mountain had turned into a real situation. On top of that, when I looked at the goat through my scope, I could see both ears but only one horn. What makes a world-record animal is the horns; if a horn had been bashed off in the fall, we'd be out of luck.

"How about we follow a trail along the river?" I asked.

"There aren't any trails along it," Heidi said.

I'd already lost the opportunity to get a goat in Alaska; I didn't want to lose this opportunity.

"The only way to get that goat," Heidi said, "is to try to work our way down through the cliffs onto that big shale slope at the bottom."

Shale slopes are no joke. A couple years back, a hunter I knew of had lost his footing and fallen to his death when he tried crossing a shale slope with a goat on his back.

We emptied our packs of everything except our rain gear, climbing gear, butchering gear, and my rifle. Grizzly bears were at the top of the food chain here, and a hungry Grizzly might very well beat us to the goat. The only thing we had going for us was that I'd shot the goat fairly early in the day, so we had a good amount of daylight to work with.

The descent took us four and a half hours. We made our way down through the cliffs and thick pine trees, skidded down the shale slope, and eventually found the goat.

It still had both horns. We got pretty ecstatic about that. Despite falling 1,800 feet, the king looked to be in pretty good shape. We took pictures, cut up the meat, which we legally had to take back with us, and put it and the pelt in game bags. All of it went into our packs, which, with the added mass, now weighed at least seventy-five pounds per person. Thank goodness Heidi had hired John, our packer, to help carry out the meat. The butchering work took about three hours to finish.

Going down hadn't been too bad on my knee but going back up was tough. The climb was dangerous, and we had to go slow. My world narrowed down to those four points of contact right in front of me. One misstep and I'd follow the same path the goat had taken down.

We made it back to the top just as full darkness fell. Working our way along the goat trail across the cliff tops, we got back to camp soaked again. The conditions had also turned miserable again, but it didn't matter. We'd gotten a Top 10 record-book mountain goat. Bagging that trophy animal was all that mattered.

It felt thrilling. It felt like I'd conquered this huge undertaking. The sense of accomplishment couldn't be beat. I made that happen. I made something happen that very few other people are able to do. Over a hundred years of hunting recordkeeping, this goat ended up being the sixth biggest ever recorded in the entire world. That's a big deal.

"Phenomenal job," I thanked Heidi. I had so much appreciation for both her skills and her own excitement. This achievement enhanced her reputation and business. Her prices went up after that.

On day four, we went back down the mountain and arrived back at base camp. From there, we went to a little dive of an airport in Telegraph Creek. Pilots and handlers for small planes often leave baggage behind because they have to be extremely cautious and specific about the amount of weight the plane carries. So I had to have a major conversation with them at the airport to make sure the goat got on the flight with me.

"Yeah, yeah," the handler I spoke with said. "No problem, no problem." His assurances didn't inspire a lot of confidence.

When I got to Vancouver to catch my connection flight, lo and behold, no goat. It had stayed back in Telegraph. The airport personnel in Vancouver told me to fly home; they'd make sure the goat got to me.

"No way," I said. "I'm staying."

I couldn't get a hotel room at the airport on the Canadian side of the border, so I crossed over into the US for the night. In the end, sorting out the shipping for the goat was a rigmarole. I went back and forth across the border four times to check whether it had finally arrived. Then, after the goat finally showed up, the American border agent made it extremely difficult for me to get back over with it, even though I had the right paperwork.

Ultimately, I did get back to Salt Lake City with the goat—and celebrated some more. Its official Boone and Crockett Score is 54 2/8. Its official Safari Club International score is 33 2/8. The two organizations use different measuring systems. When I originally shot the goat, it was number six in the world. Now, according to SCI, it has moved down to number eight in the world, just barely behind number seven. Also, on the score sheet, the scorer wrote that the horns were bigger, but a tip must have broken off in the fall. Considering part of the horn is broken off, this goat is a record-book beast.

Tracy Jacobson, the taxidermist who mounted the goat, took it to the World Taxidermy Championship where it won second place in the Full Body Taxidermy category. He also won second in the world for Large Mammal Lifesize and second in the world for the Competitors Award in the Master's Division—a truly spectacular accomplishment!

CHAPTER 10

LIVE YOUR LEGACY

I'm a very organized, proactive person. I don't let life just happen to me. I take an active role in shaping it. Every year around my birthday, I sit down and write out goals in several areas of my life that I want to accomplish. For the vast majority of my adult life, I kept up this habit.

Then I turned sixty.

It was weird.

For the first time, I struggled to map out my plans for the next one, three, five years. I had never imagined myself as a sixty-year-old. As a result, I fumbled whenever I tried to put myself in the frame of mind where I could say, "Okay, I'm sixty. This is what I'm going to do now."

I drew a blank. Living as a sixty-year-old didn't feel real. It was a very weird place to be.

What the hell? I found myself thinking. *What is my life? Where am I going?*

Mentally, I had resisted turning sixty without even realizing it. I never truly believed that a sixtieth birthday could ever arrive. I hadn't made space for that reality in my identity.

I should not be this old, I thought repeatedly. But, one day, I woke up—and I was this old. I had to confront it and figure out how to be this new person who felt like a bit of a stranger.

Hitting sixty years old is a disconcerting age. It's an age when people can no longer live in denial about their own mortality. It forces you to re-envision your life and what's next, even if you've spent years and years planning for it.

What I did *not* have to re-envision, however, was my legacy.

Legacies come in different forms:

- **Professional legacy**: This can involve building a successful career and leaving a positive impact through your business, professional endeavors, and work contributions in ways that benefit the people around you or broader society.

- **Family legacy**: This can involve passing on values, traditions, and knowledge to your children, siblings, relatives, and even parents. It can also involve philanthropy and creating a family foundation or trust to support causes that are important to your family.

- **Community legacy**: This can involve getting out into your local community and participating with intention through volunteer work, charitable giving, or activism.

- **Personal legacy**: This can involve leaving a meaningful mark, big or small, on other people through your personal relationships, mentoring, or acts of kindness.

Most people think about their legacy as something they build that will last beyond their lifetime and have a positive impact on future generations. They plan for and expect their legacy to come to fruition sometime in the future.

This is the wrong way to think about your legacy. It removes you from one of the best parts of a legacy: getting to actually experience it.

Building a legacy requires long-term vision, determination, and commitment to making a positive impact on the world. To ensure that it will be here after you're gone, you need to set goals, take action, and pay attention to the consequences that your actions may have on those who come after you. A legacy can be a source of inspiration for the people who matter most to you, the people you want to help, and future generations who will also work toward creating a better world.

All those things are true.

It's not the whole story, though. If you only envision your legacy as existing in the future, you'll find yourself working your whole life to enjoy the fruits of your labors "someday." But that day may never come, either due to your own mindset or external conditions out of your control.

So, how should you think about your legacy?

It's simple.

Don't focus on *leaving a legacy* when you're gone. *Live your legacy* in the present. It's an essential part of your life that you get to enjoy. And you do that by enjoying your life *now*, not at some vague point in the future.

"Live your legacy" is the fifth and final principle of true wealth. It played an important part in how I got through the weird experience of turning sixty. I remembered that I had been living my legacy every year leading up to my sixtieth birthday, and I would continue living it in my sixties and well beyond. I did need to put pen to paper and write out my specific goals for the next one, three, five years, but what was coming wouldn't be a huge break from what came before—because I was already living my life the way I wanted. I was born ready. I was living in alignment. I had adventure, freedom, family, gratitude, fitness and health, honesty, love, optimism, spirituality, and vision. I knew how to listen—to myself and others.

I wouldn't always be younger than sixty, and you won't be either. So what? The thirteen values of true wealth allow us to live our legacies by enjoying life and giving back.

In this chapter, I explain the importance of remembering to actually spend your money, doing the right thing for the right reason, and giving back. If you focus on these three things, you'll make sure your legacy doesn't only exist in the future for others to benefit from. You'll benefit too. And, of course, I share more hunting stories—and even explain how sharing stories is another way to give back!

Don't Forget to Spend Your Money

I often meet and work with wealthy people over age sixty. Many of them have neglected their spouse, children, or friends in their pursuit of money. They've spent their whole lives with their nose to the grindstone, achieving impressive financial success. They've accumulated and saved up all this money—more than they could ever use in their lifetime. Then, when they get older, they lift their nose from that grindstone only to discover they don't have anyone to enjoy their money with, or they don't have the health and fitness to make the most of it anymore. Some people simply don't have enough time left to enjoy the fruits of their labor fully.

Do you really have money if you can't or won't spend it?

Think of your money as food with an expiration date. If you let it sit for too long in your cupboard or refrigerator, it'll go bad. Sure, unlike food, you can save your money endlessly. It won't expire. *You* will, though. One day, you could look around and realize you have no one to cook for or share a meal with, or your doctor will seriously recommend against eating that delicious steak you can now afford for the sake of your high cholesterol.

When I tell you to spend your money, I'm not advocating for living recklessly or beyond your means. To live your legacy, enjoy your life, and give back, you have to spend your wealth responsibly. Otherwise, even if those bottom lines on your bank accounts and investment portfolios say you're rich (but you rarely, if ever, spend that wealth), then you don't actually *have* money to benefit yourself or others. You've trapped yourself in a frugal box (also known as a scarcity or poverty mindset.)

To accumulate *and* spend money, you need to create and follow a well-designed financial plan that mitigates uncertainty and gives you the freedom to spend your money according to a budget and based on the goals and vision you have for your life. You also need to resist the notion that saving your money *endlessly* will set you up for a good life. With an endlessly saving mindset, you're at risk of endlessly putting off that good life. You'll never find true wealth that way.

How do you cultivate a mindset that will allow you to spend money responsibly?

See chapter two for the seven steps you should follow to build financial wealth. These steps, and the overall learning they provide, are a great way to begin cultivating a mindset of responsible spending. Ultimately, you can't spend responsibly if you don't invest your money and let compound interest do what it does best.

There will always be uncertainty in the markets, but you can be certain of this: over time, stocks and real estate increase in value much faster than cash, bank CDs, annuities, and bonds. This is how asset classes have always worked, and the key words there are "over time." Successful investing is not a short-term endeavor, but the sooner you get started, the more opportunities you will have to grow your financial wealth.

Let's look at the history of Top Flight, one of Paragon Wealth Management's key investment portfolios. From January 1998 to March 31, 2023, Top Flight had a total return of 1,273.78 percent, compared to 576.79 percent for the S&P 500. This means that $1 million invested into Top Flight in 1998 would be worth $12,273,780 today, an increase of over twelve times the original investment. To put that in context, those returns were generated during two of the most devastating bear markets of our lifetimes.[1]

To cultivate the type of mindset you need to see these types of long-term returns, it's useful to consider the similarities between financial investing and big game hunting. Think back to my mountain goat hunts in Alaska and British Columbia (Chapters 7 and 9):

- Like our backpacks and gear on hunts, Paragon's trading systems and models are our lifeline. These models are vital to navigating our path forward and staying focused on the actual objectives of our investments.[2]

---

1 See Appendix A for disclosures, specifically item number 22.

2 See Appendix A for disclosures.

- The accumulation of snow up on those mountains is like market static—breaking news, media hype, and daily diversions. It's a distraction that can become overwhelming if we let it. This static is ubiquitous and continuously needs to be filtered through or eliminated.

- We traverse sheer cliff faces by maintaining three points of contact at all times for stability. This is how we do something risky, but in the safest way possible. The same applies for investing. We practice patience, prudence, and calculated risk, remaining focused on short- and long-term goals. We don't allow our imaginations to run wild, even when it feels like we're stuck out on a ledge, and it would be easy to succumb to panic.[3]

Financial wealth on its own won't lead you to true wealth, but it's an essential tool when you couple it with the right mindset. Don't trap yourself in a frugal box. This will prevent you from enjoying life, making a meaningful mark on our world, and helping others. Build the freedom you need to live your legacy by investing in stock and real estate—and give them time to work. But don't wait forever to spend your money. Yes, it's a tricky balance to find!

One way to find the right balance is to take breaks and vacations to renew yourself and your perspective. I always keep my 9/3 principle in mind: nine months on (work) and three months off (recreation), in whatever increments are feasible. For many people, the 9/3 principle isn't feasible during many periods of their life. But it can still be a useful goal for everyone to work toward, whether they reach it or not. Its purpose is to help you keep that idea of balance and renewal in mind, especially during stressful and fast-paced periods. When I get engaged in a project, for example, I sometimes lose the forest for the trees. Once I'm able to raise my head and look around again, I remember to go away, clear my head by doing something completely different, then come back and reengage. This helps me focus and see things I didn't before. It helps me live in the present and value the forest again.

---

3 See Appendix A for disclosures.

The 9/3 principle, and the principle of "Live your legacy" more broadly, can be especially difficult for entrepreneurs in the midst of starting a new business. The founding phase of starting a business is much like flying a small plane.

Both endeavors require building enough critical momentum to get it—the plane or the business—off the ground. Entrepreneurs have to put in these herculean efforts to make their goals and dreams a reality. They have to race ahead full throttle, even when the runway gets longer or bumpier than they expected. Taking three months off isn't an option at this stage of the entrepreneurial life cycle.

But once entrepreneurs have built the momentum they need, lifted off, and climbed to 30,000 feet, they hit cruising altitude. Now the 9/3 principle can become feasible. It's a destination to consciously work toward, and it can become a reality once you have all the critical pieces in place. Keeping the 9/3 principle in mind, using it as a compass, can help you avoid getting stuck in a never-ending, unhealthy mindset of full-throttle momentum. Humans are creatures of habit. It's easy to lose sight of what it means to actually live a good life.

So make it a priority; once you reach cruising altitude, take time to spend, rest, renew, and do the things that are most important to you outside the grind of work.

Do the Right Thing

Doing the things that are important to you is closely tied to *doing the right thing*. I first discussed this in Chapter 6 in the context of listening to your inner guide. One aspect of listening to your inner guide is doing those things that you have strong feelings of certainty about because they're the *right* thing to do—like running for mayor, even when you really don't want to.

Doing the right thing for the right reason is an integral part of living your legacy and having a positive impact beyond your own life. As with much of the wisdom I've gained in my life, it was a hunt that helped me learn this lesson. Think back to the Book Cliffs of Utah with me for one more adventure.

Catching Poachers in the Book Cliffs of Utah

One day, I got a call from the Utah Division of Wildlife Resources.

"Hey," said the woman on the telephone. "You've drawn a special tag for the Book Cliffs in our lottery system. Where should we send it?"

At first, I didn't believe her. I hadn't heard anything about a special lottery draw, so I treated it like a scam phone call. The woman and I went back and forth until she said, "If you don't want it, then we're not going to worry about it."

"No," I said, laughing a bit but still skeptical. "If it's real, I want it."

I still wasn't convinced she'd actually called from the Division of Wildlife Resources until the tag showed up in my mail.

The Division of Wildlife Resources regulates hunting in Utah depending on how high they're trying to keep the quality of its animal populations. If they need to increase the number of deer in a particular area, they issue fewer tags for it.

I had hunted the Book Cliffs before when it was an open area, but I hadn't been back since the state had locked it down. That made it more difficult to get a tag through the standard application process, but it improved the quality of deer that hunters were able to take. To get higher quality bucks, they have to live five to eight years. That's when they reach their full maturity and potential.

My youngest son Austin, a fun-loving ten year-old at the time who lived to go hunting, helped me pack and load our four-wheeler and all our gear into our camping trailer. Together, we headed out to the Book Cliffs.

For the first four days, we had a great time hunting and camping. On the fifth day, Austin stayed back with the trailer while I went out alone. I decided to make a serious go of it, so I geared up in a full ghillie suit, a Sasquatch type of clothing designed to camouflage a stationary person into their environment. Military snipers use ghillie suits.

I spent the morning watching and glassing the terrain around me, quietly enjoying myself. After a few hours, I spotted a solid 4-point buck that most people would be very excited to shoot. It wasn't the quality of buck I was looking for, but I kept an eye on it while it moved across the sagebrush canyon floor below me.

A full-sized Ford Bronco appeared off in the distance, slowly cruising down the dirt road. Alone in my ghillie suit, they didn't see me sitting above them on the hill in some nearby bushes. They did see the deer, though. Four men jumped out of the Bronco, all armed with muzzleloaders.

Well, this is not normal, I thought.

Since the Book Cliffs had become a special draw area, four people in a group should not have had a gun. Sure, four-man hunting parties aren't out of the ordinary. But I would've expected only one, *maybe* two, to be armed while the others came as support. Everyone with a gun would have legally needed a tag. The Book Cliffs area was just too difficult to draw a tag in for all four hunters to have gotten one.

The four men fired at the deer, killing it.

Then they raced over to it. Instead of taking their time and gutting the deer like typical hunters would do, they each grabbed the animal by a hoof, hauled it to the Bronco, and threw it in the back. Obviously in a hurry, they piled back into the Bronco, turned around, and drove off, like a bat out hell at close to 60 mph.

I hiked back to where I'd stashed my four-wheeler and took off after the Bronco. They had pulled quite a way ahead of me, but I followed the dust trail they left in their wake as they sped along. Once they arrived at their camp, I made my way onto a shelf above them, out of sight and a fair distance away.

Austin and I had set up our camp only three-quarters of a mile away.

The men pulled the deer out of the back of the Bronco and began cutting it up. Two of them dug a hole and started throwing the guts in it. After watching their progress for a while, I pulled out my cell phone. No service.

Hiking up the mountain at my back, my phone got cell service once I'd reached the top. Hurriedly, I put in a call to the closest Division of Wildlife Resources office, in Vernal, Utah.

"I've seen some poachers," I told the woman who answered. "You need to send an officer. This needs to be investigated."

After telling her everything I'd seen, she said, "That's interesting. Now, where are you, exactly?"

As we talked, I remember thinking she seemed a little stiff, like she was distracted or maybe withholding something. It just wasn't a fluid conversation.

I gave her the GPS locations of the poachers' camp and my camp with Austin, expecting someone to show up to talk to me the next day.

And that, I figured, would be that. A group of poachers out to illegally take a buck's trophy-sized antlers would be held accountable. I went back to my four-wheeler and returned to Austin.

The next day, nobody came to see me.

What the heck is going on? I thought, getting frustrated. *Why are they dragging their feet?*

Another day passed. Most hunters would have let it go at that point. I didn't have to do anything more; Austin and I had been distracted from our own hunt enough. But poachers are horrible people. They take precious wildlife resources and waste them. Poaching is not okay in my book.

I hiked back up the mountain to get cell service and called the Division of Wildlife Resources office again.

"Hey," I said to a different employee. "I've got an issue. I made a report two days ago. I haven't seen anyone. What's going on?"

"Huh?" said the employee. "That's unusual. We don't have a record of it."

"Well, I reported this to a colleague of yours, a woman. That's all I know about her."

"That's really weird." After I repeated the entire experience, he said, "We'll get an officer out there right away."

The next day, an officer named Jason Teeguarden came out to our trailer. Austin listened in as we spoke, curious about what would happen to these poachers.

"The woman you must have spoken to took off," Jason told me. "She hasn't been in the office for three days."

"Are those her regular days off?" I asked.

"No, she said she had to take care of something personal."

Jason went to the four men's camp. Luckily, they hadn't left yet. When he came back, Jason told me, "I think there's been a misunderstanding. You know, these are good guys. We know who they are. They wouldn't poach anything. So, it's all good. Don't worry about it."

"No," I said bluntly. "I saw them shoot the deer. I'll show you where they shot it. And when they leave their camp, I'll show you where they buried the deer guts. You can take DNA from both spots and match the samples."

"Well, I really don't think there's anything going on. But, you know, if you're going to push it, we can go out there."

We hiked to where the deer had been killed. The tracks were clear, but it took some effort to find useable blood because the men had carried the deer out without dragging it. Jason retrieved the samples and loaded them into his DNA kit.

Because the men hadn't left their camp yet, Jason planned to stay in the general area and wait them out. I went back to camp with Austin.

The next morning, Austin and I woke up to the four poachers raising hell in our camp. Austin stayed in the trailer, worried, but trusting I'd take care of the situation. I went out and stood on the trailer's metal step with my muzzleloader.

The men cursed me out. They yelled. They threatened.

"You didn't see anything."

"You imagined it."

"You're a horrible person for turning us in."

"You're just creating problems."

Unimpressed, I told them to go to hell.

"Get out of here!" I said. "I saw what I saw. Poaching is crap."

They didn't scare me. They pissed me off.

Eventually, the men packed up and left.

Jason returned, and we went over to their camp. I showed him where they'd buried the deer guts, and he took samples from that as well. Jason also told me that the woman I'd originally spoken to from the Division of Wildlife Resources office was married to one of the poachers. After my report, she drove out to their camp and told them. On top of that, I learned that one of the other men in the hunting party worked as a police officer in Vernal.

Once Jason had everything he needed, Austin and I spent a couple more days hunting. I even got a nice buck that scored 187.

The saga didn't end there, of course. The woman I spoke to remained on duty while the investigation slowly progressed. Getting DNA test results takes time, and she could access all my contact information that the Division of Wildlife Resources had in its system.

I received harassing phone calls and voicemails telling me to drop this and go away. I didn't share the details with my family, wanting to protect them from any unnecessary worry. I wrote an affidavit describing everything that I'd seen and submitted it for the investigation. Eventually, the DNA samples came back a match. With my testimony and those results, the Division of Wildlife Resources took the four men to court. I was told by the Vernal office that they all lost their hunting privileges. What other consequences they faced, such as fines, I never found out.

Jason had originally trusted the men because he knew them. He genuinely believed at first that there had been some sort of misunderstanding. Once I gave him irrefutable evidence, however, he pushed the prosecution forward.

Later, I found out that when you turn in a poacher and they get prosecuted, the Division of Wildlife Resources rewards you with another tag. So, the next year, Austin and I headed out to the Book Cliffs again.

During our first hunt to the Book Cliffs, when I'd drawn a regular tag, I'd taken an exceptional buck that scored 196. That second buck I got scored 187. On our third trip to the Book Cliffs, I got another good buck that scored 185. Sticking it to a group of poachers—including a cop and the spouse of a Division of Wildlife Resources employee, no less—was the cherry on top. Austin couldn't have agreed more. A serious little hunter, he thought poachers were garbage too.

Austin is still very into hunting today, but he's not so little anymore. When he was in grade school, I'd come home from work to find him on the couch with a hunting show on TV and all my hunting magazines and trip photos spread around him.

This experience became a valuable lesson for Austin—and for me. I taught all my kids that it's important to do the right thing for the right reason and let the consequences follow, whatever they may be. Sometimes you also have to buck authority—whether it's a Division of Wildlife Resources officer, an expert in your field, a parent giving you advice, or someone else—and push to make something happen when you know you're right. This is what it looks like to live your legacy.

Give Back and Serve Others

There are a lot of ways to give back. They may be big or small. They may or may not receive recognition from others. As long as they are meaningful to you, they contribute to your legacy.

Giving back starts at home. It can be as simple (or as complicated) as valuing and taking care of your family relationships. My role as a husband, father, and grandfather will always be fundamental to how I give back. As a family, we especially value giving back to our community together through our Live Your Dream Foundation by awarding scholarships to single mothers attending any educational opportunity that will increase their earning potential to better provide for their families. Anything from a boot camp to a full university education within the state of Utah is included. I continue to provide support for the organization's fundraising activities, including sponsoring its annual golf tournament through Paragon.

The connection between the Live Your Dream Foundation, Paragon, and my family is an enormous source of pride and legacy for me. Not only does my daughter Katie lead the organization and donate all her time, but Paragon also provides financial support and donates staff time. This support and donated time allows almost 100 percent of the funds raised to go toward scholarships and other gifts, like school supplies, Thanksgiving meals, Christmas support, Mother's Day baskets, and more.

I foster this commitment to giving back at Paragon by ensuring we have family-friendly employee policies. Employees can leave work to attend family activities, and we encourage them to actively engage in the community. We all believe in educating our community and the general public about complicated investment topics. Our educational resources have been used by investors, students, and other Americans across the country.

At the beginning of this chapter, I described how, every year, I write out goals in several areas of my life that I want to accomplish. Consider using this type of exercise to brainstorm and organize how you currently give back or want to give back in your own life. As a starting point and framework, you can use the four types of legacy that I introduced earlier in this chapter (professional, family, community, and personal), or you can identify your own set of areas that mean the most to you.

This type of list doesn't only help you envision, re-envision, and plan the legacy you want to live. It also helps you track and celebrate everything you accomplish. In my role as mayor of Orem, I pay close attention to my long list of goals. That way, as a leader, I know exactly how much progress our city is making. This also keeps me accountable to the city and citizens whom I serve.

Consider the "Mayor and Orem City Council Focus" list that I've included here to capture what we've accomplished during my first twenty-one months as mayor from January 2022 to September 2023. I'm sharing this list with you to illustrate what you, too, can accomplish when you write out your goals and track your progress. Regularly updating this list has helped me know where I and the Orem City Council stand as we work to improve the quality of life in Orem.

Our city attorney, who has been with us for twenty-two years, says he has never seen anything close to this level of activity. Likewise, previous city council members say we have done more in twenty months than was done in the past twelve years. That type of positive feedback confirms for me that we're making a difference for Orem. It also motivates me to keep going, especially during times when the going gets tough.

Mayor and Orem City Council Focus
First Twenty-One Months
January 2022–September 2023

VALUES AND VISION

Purpose: To create an environment where families can thrive. We want Orem to be the best place to raise a family in America.

Orem Core Values: God, Family, Country

In God We Trust
We passed a resolution designating our official city motto as "In God We Trust."

- We will be the second city in Utah to adopt this as our official motto.
- The motto will be placed on our Orem City Seal, Orem City Council Chambers, and new Orem City Center.

Family City USA is officially designated as the Orem City Brand.

- Installed at city entrances, buildings, vehicles, and public parks.
- Created a new Orem City, Family City USA flag for use throughout the city.
- Passed an ordinance defining which flags can be flown on city property.
- Our city Summerfest celebration was renamed Oremfest with a family focus.
- Going forward, "Family City USA" is the benchmark by which all City Council Legislative decisions are measured.

Freedom Pavilion

- A patriotic pavilion honoring our country is being built next to the new City Center.
- It will have a Gold Star Family Memorial.

(continues on next page)

RETURNED REPRESENTATION TO THE PEOPLE OF OREM

Re-established the Legislative Authority of the City Council
- Restructured the mayor and city council from a primarily ceremonial role to being the actual legislative body accountable to the citizens.
- Adopted new processes and rules for the operation of the city council.
- Passed a resolution giving the council the right to hire a full-time attorney.
- Restored citizen control of the planning commission and other citizen commissions.

Aligned the City Council and City Management
- To better represent Orem citizens.
- Hired an outstanding new city manager.
- The new management structure is more cost-effective and efficient.
- Employees are excited about the changes and new opportunities created.

GREEN SPACE PROTECTION

Orem Land Preservation Act Established
- A majority of the City council voted to protect and preserve all school building land, public parks, and publicly-owned property throughout Orem via a city-wide zoning change.
- This protects our green space and school properties from being sold or developed for purposes other than their original intent.

WATER CONSERVATION AND ENHANCEMENT

Orem's Water Reuse Conservation Project—Under Construction
- This **$20 million project reduces** Orem's water consumption **by 10% (effectively a decrease of 10,000 people)** without negatively affecting our residents.
- The mayor personally obtained $10 million in grants for this project.
- The Orem City staff obtained $3 million in grants. These grants saved taxpayers **$13 million.**
- No new taxes.

Heritage Park—Under Construction
- This **new $32 million park** improves our water infrastructure and helps us prepare for the future by constructing a **950-foot well** and a **ten-million-gallon** water tank buried under the park.
- No new taxes.

FAMILY FRIENDLY INFRASTRUCTURE

State Street Master Plan Major Overhaul—Stage 1
- City council focused on responsible growth and **eliminated 10,000** high-density multifamily apartments on State Street.
- Focus is now on service, office, and retail development.
- Prioritized protection of family neighborhoods near high-density rental apartments.
- Require adequate infrastructure and parking.
- Maintain reasonable traffic flows and business access.

(continues on next page)

New State-of-the-Art City Center—Under Construction

- This was talked about for years but never moved forward. Now it is being built. Most importantly, this **$30 million dollar facility** is being built using existing funds.
- No tax increases or bonding to pay for this project.

Hillcrest Park—Under Construction

- This **amazing new $12 million park** preserves a portion of Hillcrest Elementary to serve as a community center and will feature a splash pad, twelve pickleball courts, and playgrounds.
- No new taxes.

Lakeview Park

- The mayor and city staff worked together to **save Orem taxpayers $2 million** on this project to add infield and outfield turf and lights for its softball fields.
- This allows the fields to be used year-round and the city to host regional tournaments.
- No new taxes.

FISCAL RESPONSIBILITY AND TAX SAVINGS

Operational Savings

- City executive management staff members were replaced as needed.
- **Reduced** city payroll costs **$1,903,000** during the first six months of 2023.
- Created **new positions ($795,000)** to upgrade and enhance public services.
- **Net ongoing savings** to taxpayers of **$1,108,000 annually**.

Taxes and Fees

- There have been **NO city-implemented tax increases since taking office.**

- Orem taxpayers learned they would **pay $116 million and receive only $16 million** in benefits from the proposed school bond and voted it down.
- Accessory Dwelling Apartment's annual licensing fee was eliminated.
- Mayor lobbied the county against a new 0.2% sales tax increase.
- **Orem's utility fees are currently the lowest in Utah County.**

Tax Imbalance—Alpine School District

- After learning about a negative $174 million tax imbalance and talking about reconfiguration for twenty years, the **Orem City Council finally voted to "allow" their citizens to vote** on whether or not to split from Alpine School District.

Orem Emergency Dispatch Center combined with Provo City

- Lowers costs and improves services for both cities.

Taxpayer Savings through Grants Received

- **$21,082,759** total grants applied for and received.
- **$7,604,213** additional grants pending.

TRANSPARENCY AND LISTENING

Orem Transparency Portal

- Provides a newly created, first-ever, one-stop transparency portal for residents to see what their elected officials are doing and how they vote.
- Provides **a new level of transparency** to hold city officials accountable.

The Citizens Voice Portal—Under Construction

- This new portal will **allow our citizens to be heard.**
- This will be a place for citizens to voice their concerns and make suggestions about any issues affecting our city.

(continues on next page)

EMPLOYEES

Employee Survey Results

In-depth, anonymous city employee survey completed July 2023:

- **95%** Survey participation rate of full-time employees
- **80%** Orem is headed in the right direction
- **92%** City leaders lead with integrity
- **80%** Motivated at the start of each day
- **93%** Right tools and resources to execute their job

Comprehensive City Management and Operations Evaluation—In Process

- The most extensive review and survey of all city management and operations ever done by a city government in Utah.
- Our objective is to optimize all areas of our city government.
- We want to provide our residents with the best and most cost-effective services and provide city employees with a great work environment.

RECENT RECOGNITION

Livable Cities Award

- In 2023, Livability examined 2,300 cities using 100 data points and designated Orem as one of the Top 100 Best Places to Live in America.

Milken Award

- In 2023, Provo-Orem was ranked first for best-performing large city in the 2023 Milken Institute Best-Performing Cities Index.

Telling Stories to Give Back

Find ways to give back and serve others in ways that fall within your control and align with the legacy you want to live. The stories I've been telling in this book are, for several reasons, one more way I'm able to give back. First, people who know me and the adventures I've been on have been asking me to write these stories down and share them for years now. Second, the parallels between big game hunting, financial investing, and that deeper and richer experience of true wealth are worth exploring. We can all learn from these parallels and use them to better our lives and legacies. Third, these stories allow me to recognize and show gratitude for the people who have come on thrilling and challenging adventures with me, who have hunted for true wealth with me, and who live legacies that have left meaningful impacts on me.

So, to end this chapter, I'd like to share one more story to honor my friend Nathan Ricks, a brilliant man who left us too soon.

Hunting Mule Deer on Buckhorn Ranch

In the fall of 2010, I spent nine noncontinuous days deer hunting on my friend Nathan Ricks' 6,000-acre family ranch in Utah with a couple hundred grass-fed cows. Hunting used to be common in the area before Nathan bought the ranch, but due to overhunting, he had cut the number of hunters way back several years prior.

Nathan didn't hunt, but he didn't hesitate to let me use the land. "Yeah, you can go up and hunt Buckhorn Ranch. That's fine. I trust you."

I arrived at Nathan's awesome cabin on Buckhorn Ranch, about twenty-plus miles past Strawberry Reservoir and up Currant Creek Canyon. The original cabin, dating back to the first pioneers who settled on the land, still stood nearby. The cold and snow amplified the quiet, making everything feel pristine and untouched.

I dove right into hunting the mountainous canyons. The land was covered with a mix of sagebrush and red rock. As you work your way up a mountain and gain elevation, you make your way into quakies and pines. From what I could tell, it had some, but not much, hunting pressure. If a deer stumbled into the path of a casual hunter on a four-wheeler, and they wanted to shoot it, they would. But serious trophy hunters certainly hadn't been coming up and hunting the area methodically.

Because I lived within a hundred miles of Buckhorn Ranch, I spent three to four days in the cabin at a time throughout the fall months. Sometimes I brought Shawn and Austin with me; other times I went alone.

Over the course of the hunt, I spotted several really nice mule deer bucks that would've satisfied most hunters. I was looking for something better. Much better. I wanted a monster and was willing to hunt as long as it took. It was go big or go home empty-handed.

Early one morning, after nine days of hunting, I climbed up to a peak surrounded by cliffs. A mile away, I saw two giant bucks on the other side of a huge canyon. They worked their way through the snow that had fallen the night before. Excited, I pulled out my binoculars to see them better.

Both deer appeared to be beautiful, gigantic, perfect bucks. In a perfect box frame, the first buck's antlers likely had eleven points and were thirty-one inches across. The second buck's antlers were even wider, at thirty-five inches across. That's phenomenal for a deer. One side of the second buck's antlers were super thick, almost webbed, while the other side had six points.

I stared across the canyon at these two monsters—and went nuts inside.

This is why we do this, I thought.

The pair bedded down around nine o'clock that morning. I took my time really dialing them in. Because of the distance between us, I had to pay close attention to make sure I knew where they went once they'd disappeared from sight.

Hustling back to Buckhorn Ranch, I looped in Ryan, the ranch manager. "I need you to come up the mountain and help guide me to where these deer are," I explained.

Ryan enthusiastically lent a hand—or, in this case, his eyes. We climbed back up. Ryan took a position near where I'd originally been standing when I saw the deer. It took me almost two hours to get down the canyon and halfway up the other side.

Throughout the trek, I kept Ryan in sight and looked back at him periodically through my binoculars. He gave me hand signals telling me which way to go.

I knew I'd reached the general area where the deer had bedded when I started recognizing the terrain. Pulling out a small tube of baby powder, I sent a small puff into the air to check the direction of the slight breeze. As I approached the location of the deer, I made sure the breeze was always blowing into my face, so they'd be less likely to smell me.

Finally, after what seemed forever, only 120 yards of quakies separated us. I could see the antlers of one of the giant bucks, but I couldn't see the other one.

Ever so slowly, I got myself a dead rest and trained my rifle scope on the one bedded deer that I could see.

He stood up.

I moved my point of aim right behind his shoulder.

Animals have amazing instincts. Their senses of smell and hearing are vastly superior to humans. They can feel your presence and attention on them. And it's obvious when that awareness has kicked in, even if they haven't looked right at you. Even if you've stayed out of sight and kept the wind blowing toward you.

In most big game hunts like this, whoever sees the other first—animal or human—wins. If I see the animal first, I've increased my odds a ton and have a leg up on getting as close as I can to him. If he sees, smells, or hears me first, I'm screwed.

You have to win that game.

I held the crosshairs of my scope right behind the shoulder of the standing buck, but I wanted to see the other buck before pulling the trigger. I suspected the second buck was the bigger of the two. I kept staying on the first buck standing motionless for about sixty seconds. All of a sudden, I felt a breeze on the back of my neck.

The direction of the wind had reversed.

The buck tensed up, ready to explode into action.

I squeezed the trigger. The buck went down.

The second buck jumped up, taking off along a ridge fifty yards below me and looking straight at me. I had my rifle on him and desperately wanted to pull the trigger. But I only had one tag, which meant I could only shoot one buck. Off he went.

I hiked up to where the buck had fallen and confirmed what a phenomenal animal he was. He was magnificent, right at thirty-one inches across, with a box frame that had the deepest forks I'd ever seen. If you're into numbers, he scored 208. He was a classic four-by-four with extra points on each side and two eye guards. If you were to check how a hunting textbook defines the perfect buck, this would be it—a vision of perfection.

The following year, I returned to Buckhorn Ranch and spent an entire trip trying to find that second monster deer again. I never did. A predator or bad weather likely killed him as he passed from peak maturity into old age. But he lives forever in my memory, and Buckhorn Ranch will always have a special place in my heart.

Nathan Ricks and I knew each other for thirty-five years. We invested together, grew our careers together, and became good friends. On January 2, 2023, as I was writing this book, Nathan died in a plane crash. That fall, I'd been talking regularly with Nathan about an investment project we were investing together on. He was an internationally recognized business leader, network marketer, public speaker, and one of the largest commercial real estate developers in Utah. More importantly, Nathan was a husband, a father of four daughters, a grandfather to fifteen beautiful grandchildren, and a community leader driven to serve others.

Nathan lived life to the fullest. He was one of those bright lights that make the world a better place. He'll be seriously missed. His passing reminds me to focus on what really matters and make every day count. Nathan embodied what it means to live your legacy *now*, in the present, and hunt for true wealth every day of your life.

Don't waste any more time. Control what you can control. Make this year better than last year. Make next year better than this year. Figure out what makes you happy, go get it, and always give back. Live your legacy.

HUNTING ELK IN NEW MEXICO, LUCKY NUMBER 13

Over the course of my life, I've spent at least a thousand nights out in the backcountry, much of that time hunting. What have I learned from all that experience? You have to practice the fundamentals. Fundamentals are everything in hunting, investing, and in life.

In 2008, I decided to go on an elk hunt in New Mexico. It was September 22, a beautiful fall in the gold and tan-colored mountains of New Mexico. Brown grasses covered the desert landscape dotted with tree cholla cactus, piñon pine, and green juniper shrubs that reached to the top of each rocky mesa.

Now, to really get this story, you need to know about my lucky number.

A bit paradoxically, or at least ironically, 13 is my lucky number. It pops up in my life *all the time*. When I was younger, I thought it would bring me bad luck. I'd get annoyed when it kept appearing over and over and over. Hotel rooms, house addresses, invoices and receipts, financials, and so much more. Eventually, though, I got fed up and embraced it as my own. Even my staff are aware of it and point out whenever a significant 13 makes an appearance.

On this particular trip to New Mexico, I decided to go hunt on the Acoma Pueblo Indian Reservation located in Unit 13. To manage the state's big game species, the New Mexico Department of Game and Fish divides the land into game management units. A couple years before, I'd killed a good elk in this same unit.

I rushed to the airport and snapped a photo of the parking spot so I could find my car when I returned. It happened to be in row 13. I went to the shuttle bus stop, and that read "Stop 13." Next, the airport terminal gate had 13 in it. Then, my seat on the airplane was in row 13. In New Mexico, the SUV I rented had 13,200 miles on it.

Driving out to Unit 13, I could not have been more convinced that this was going to be a phenomenal hunt.

I got to the reservation in the evening and met up with my local guide, Robert, and a few other hunters and guides who'd also arrived. They'd already set up a small camp in a clearing in the woods with canvas white wall tents, so we passed a good night together.

"I just got here, but see that guy over there?" Robert asked, as he pointed to a tall guy with blond hair and a ponytail. "He's been here for twelve days. He keeps going to the same spot every time." Usually, a group of hunters would come in and hunt for five to six days. Then they'd take off, and the next group would come in.

I went over and introduced myself, discovering that Jim, a bow hunter, was disgusted. "This is a joke. I've hunted hard, and there's nothing out here. I'm sick of this place."

"Well, we don't have anywhere to take Dave tomorrow," said Robert. "Would it be okay if he goes out to where you've been hunting?"

Jim shrugged dismissively. "Yeah, sure. I mean, you're wasting your time, but you can go out there if you want. It's stupid. I shouldn't have stayed here this long."

Jim decided to stay one more day before leaving.

The following morning, Robert had to go check out some other hunting spots. Before sunrise, he dropped me off where Jim had been twiddling his thumbs for almost two weeks. We arrived at a large pond.

"Be careful," Robert said to me as I got out of his truck in the dark. "I'll be back tonight to pick you up." On this type of hunt, the animals are most active during the first and last hours of light, so you stay out all day if you're far enough out that you don't have time to get back and forth to your camp.

I made my way around the pond and got myself set up in a patch of brush and shrub that I could hide in. Big game hunts typically take me about eight to nine days to put a trophy on the ground. That's my average. Not surprisingly, then, I settled in ready for an uneventful first day.

Off in the distance, I heard a bugle, the signature call of a bull that bulls use to call cows and gather their herd.

All right, cool, I thought. *At least one elk is out here.*

I bugled back at the bull. It had to be at least half a mile away, if not farther. Some distance from the pond, the land rose into a small hill, then dipped into a canyon. A ravine flowed through the far side of it. The bull had to be somewhere beyond that.

The bull and I bugled back and forth, and slowly it started to draw closer. This continued for over an hour. I had no idea if it would turn out to be a tiny bull or the giant bull I was after. I stayed on high alert, but I also didn't feel a lot of optimism. Jim's complaints about how much this area sucked rang in my ears.

A cow elk came trotting over the small hill. Then about twenty feet behind her, a bull followed.

Holy shiz, I thought. *He's a monster.*

I had a muzzleloader, which only shoots accurately so far, because New Mexico restricts rifle permits in order to control the big game hunting in the area. Success rates with this type of weapon are much lower, making the hunt that much more challenging—and potentially more rewarding if I could get a good animal.

When I first laid eyes on the bull, about 250 yards separated us. I put my shooting sticks in place, which is essentially a small, very portable tripod. I'd learned long ago that the key to making a good shot is to have perfect stability. If you shoot at 100 yards with a muzzleloader, and you jerk the tiniest bit to the left, say a half of an inch or so, you're going to be two feet off the target.

I got set up on the shooting sticks and watched the elk come closer. The cow stayed in front of the bull. They made it all the way to the other side of the pond.

Oh crap, oh crap, I thought about the cow the whole time. *Don't turn too soon. Don't turn too soon.*

If she turned, the bull would follow her, so he wouldn't come within range of me. With that much distance between us, any number of trees, shrubs, and big rocks could also get in the way. A thousand things could go wrong that would cause this to not work out.

I kept focused and patient. As soon as the bull turned, he gave me his right shoulder.

I squeezed off a shot.

Boom.

The bull tumbled backward, away from the pond. He went down instantly, and I could tell I'd hit him right where I'd been aiming. The cow disappeared into the wilderness.

I had my own little private celebration. Something amazing had just happened. But I also had to work through a bit of shock at how sudden it had all happened.

I couldn't be sure yet how big the bull was, but I knew he was one of the biggest elk I'd ever seen. Gathering up my gear, I headed over to him and had another little celebration before caping and cleaning him out.

That night, Robert returned. "Okay, you ready to go?"

I pointed into the dark. "Yeah, I got an elk over there."

"Really?" When Robert saw the elk, he was shocked too. He went nuts over its size. An average big elk will score between 320 and 350 points. Everyone will talk about a 350-point elk. This bull would officially end up scoring 400 4/8. According to Safari Club International at the time, he ranked third in the world in the SCI record book for a trophy elk taken with a muzzleloader. Over fifteen years later, this elk slipped just one spot down to rank fourth in the world in the muzzleloader category.

It took a while to get him loaded in the truck, but we finally finished and headed back to camp. Jim was not happy to say the least.

It turned out, my first day on this hunt would have been Jim's thirteenth day—my lucky number.

I showed up at the same place another hunter had been going to for almost two weeks. At that point, I had a lot of experience hunting, so despite hearing Jim's complaints about the location, I simply stuck to the fundamentals: I got to the location early, checked the wind, stayed focused, kept being patient, and waited for the elk to make a mistake, so I could execute. Even if this spot had frustrated another hunter, I also trusted my own instincts when they said to go ahead and check out the same spot. I checked the wind again and bugled and cow called back and forth patiently, despite not knowing what size animal I was communicating with. Quickly but calmly, I set up a stable shot.

You never know what's going to happen next in life. You just have to master and keep doing the fundamentals so that these brilliant moments—whether they're gifts from God, great karma from lucky number 13, or something else—can come together perfectly.

An elk could have just as easily *not* shown up for me that day. Because you don't know; you never really know. The only way you win battles like these is to simply keep doing what you know to do and do it consistently over time by showing up yourself.

Throughout this book, I've been your guide to true wealth, showing you how I have practiced the five principles of true wealth in my own life: (1) Go big or go home, (2) Build solid relationships; value your family, friends, and community, (3) Don't panic; things go wrong, (4) Expect bear markets; be positioned for bull markets, and (5) Live your legacy now.

You, too, can achieve true wealth by practicing these fundamentals in the context of your own life, your own passions, and your own relationships—all you've got to do is believe! That slogan comes from my magic days when people endlessly asked me how I did magic. I would always pause and suck them in a little bit, making them think I might actually tell them how. Then I'd say, "All you've got to do is believe." I'd also keep a small sign with that message on one of my magic tables.

Every time I did a big show, I'd set it out for myself to look at and keep me in that magical mindset.

Over the years since I performed as a magician, I've always preached that if you want to do something everyone else says is impossible—start a business, go on a trophy hunt, or pursue any dream you've been dreaming—you have to start with "all you've got to do is believe!" Now, I obviously believe fulfilling a dream takes much more than just believing, but at the same time, actually believing something is possible is the foundation for achieving anything great. You must be optimistic and believe. You must think you can overcome any obstacles in the face of all the people who will tell you that what you're trying can't be done. Believing is not the entire solution, but it's an important first step, and it's where my mind goes whenever I'm going down a difficult path and hitting obstacles. At times like those, I tell myself, "All you've got to do is believe!"

Remember, too, that achieving financial wealth is just one aspect of living an optimistic life of true wealth. The straightest path to true wealth is about staying aligned with your values. It's about focusing on the quality of your life—both the ups and the downs. And it's about contributing to other people's lives too. Whenever your life goes sideways (and it will), you now know that's your opportunity and responsibility to take your life back.

As I got older, however, I found myself just saying NO to invitations to go places or do things more often because I felt too busy. NO became the easiest way to take my life back, or so it seemed. After thinking about the number of NO's I was saying, I realized I was missing out on some of the joy of basic interactions with other people because I was focused on completing my never-ending list of projects that had to get done. Then I thought about the government campaign against drugs: "Just Say No." From that ubiquitous slogan, I noticed that out of habit, people like me seemed to be saying, "Just Say No" too often and losing out on some of life's happiness.

Realistically, you *do* have to pick between opportunities because you don't have unlimited time. But in the context of living a full life of true wealth, try "Just Say Yes" more often than not. I've found that living my crazy busy life—especially since "mayor" got added to the mix—it's surprising and fulfilling to see just how much a person as busy as me is capable of dreaming and actually doing with the right people and support systems in place.

Ultimately, the promise of hunting for true wealth—deep happiness and fulfillment—is a lifelong experience of living your legacy now, in the present moment, for yourself and the people you love.

I invite you to get to it!

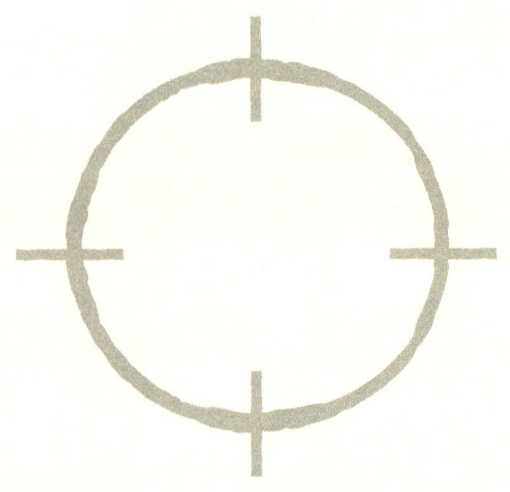

ACKNOWLEDGMENTS

Several years ago, my daughter Shannon told me I "must" write a book. Then more recently, Laura Bush, Founder of Peacock Proud Press and a long-time client of mine, pushed harder and told me these amazing stories would be gone forever if I didn't put them in a book soon. I'm grateful for Shannon and Laura's persistence in pushing me to make this happen. It's exciting to see this dream become a reality.

I especially want to thank my wife, Cathy. She's very independent and always there for me. She's also a great partner I love very much and supports me in everything I do. To say we've had an adventurous forty-four years together is a vast understatement.

I want to thank our five children and my grandchildren for the love, support, and joy they bring into my life. Raising them has crystalized who I am and refined my beliefs about what I believe the essence of true wealth to be. My family is the center of my life.

A very special thanks to Sarai Hess, my executive assistant at Paragon, and Tess Jones, my executive assistant at Orem City. These two amazing women work together to make my life happen. They are indispensable and deserve credit for a lot of what I can accomplish.

Thank you to Nathan White, KaNeil Menlove, and my team at Paragon Wealth Management for their critical roles in delivering our services at Paragon. My team's professional skills and high-quality customer service have enabled me to continue leading the business, become the Mayor of Orem, take extended hunting trips worldwide, and spend precious time with my family. Also, most importantly, a very special thank you to our clients for entrusting us with their life savings, which defines their future.

Thank you to Orem City Council members, Executive Staff, and Orem City employees for supporting the re-establishment of Orem as "Family City USA." It's an honor and a privilege to serve as your mayor and a catalyst for positive change in our community. I'm particularly grateful to our 1,100 plus full and part-time employees who work hard to make Orem the best it can be.

Thank you to the many friends and guides I have met along the way on these extreme adventures pursuing "monster" trophy animals.

Special thanks to Laura Bush, PhD, and her team at Peacock Proud Press for all their hard work and excellent writing and publishing skills to help me bring this book together. I could not have done this without them. They have helped me live my legacy now by making this book a reality.

APPENDIX A
DISCLOSURES

Any information contained in this book is for informational purposes only and is not intended as an offer or solicitation with respect to the purchase or sale of any security. Investments in securities involve the risk of loss. Past performance is no guarantee of future results. All opinions and estimates included in this correspondence constitute the judgment as of the dates indicated and are subject to change without notice. Do not rely upon this information to predict future investment performance or market conditions. This information is not a substitute for consultation with a competent financial, legal, or tax advisor and should only be used in conjunction with his/her advice.

Rankings and recognitions by unaffiliated publications should not be construed by a client or prospective client as a guarantee that Paragon Wealth Management will provide a certain level of results in client accounts, nor should they be construed as current or past endorsements of Paragon Wealth Management by clients. Such publications base their selections on information prepared and/or submitted by the recognized entities.

This book may contain forward-looking statements that involve known and unknown risks, uncertainties, and other factors which may cause the actual results, performance, or achievements of the company to be materially different from any future results, performance, or achievements expressed or implied in such forward-looking statements. The most significant of these factors include, but are not limited to, the following: the performance of financial markets, the investment performance of sponsored investment products and separately managed accounts, general economic conditions, industry trends, future acquisitions, competitive conditions, and government regulations.

1. Author Qualifications

I, Dave Young, am the founder and president of Paragon Wealth Management and have thirty-seven years of experience in the financial industry. This book is based on my knowledge and expertise gained throughout my career.

2. No Personalized Advice

This book is intended for general informational purposes only and should not be considered personalized financial advice. Each individual's financial situation is unique, and you should consult with a qualified financial professional before making any investment decisions.

3. Disclosure of Conflicts of Interest

I may have financial interests in certain investment products or services mentioned in this book. I am committed to providing unbiased information, but readers should be aware of potential conflicts of interest. I will not recommend any product or service solely for my personal gain.

4. Investment Risks

Investing involves risks, and past performance is not indicative of future results. The information provided in this book does not guarantee any specific investment outcomes. Readers should carefully consider their risk tolerance and investment objectives.

5. Legal and Regulatory Compliance

This book complies with all relevant financial regulations and laws applicable at the time of publication. However, financial regulations may change over time, and readers are responsible for ensuring their compliance with current laws and regulations.

6. Consult a Professional

Readers are strongly encouraged to consult with a qualified financial advisor or legal professional before making any financial decisions. The information in this book is not a substitute for professional advice tailored to your specific circumstances.

7. Disclaimer on Market Predictions

Any predictions or forecasts about the financial markets or economic conditions mentioned in this book are based on information available at the time of writing and are subject to change. No one can predict future market movements with certainty.

8. No Endorsement of Products or Services

Mention of specific financial products, services, or companies in this book does not constitute an endorsement. Readers should conduct their own research and due diligence before considering any investment or financial product.

9. Limitation of Liability

The author and publisher are not responsible for any actions or decisions made by readers based on the information in this book. The information is provided as-is, without any warranties or guarantees.

10. Updating Information

Financial markets and regulations can change rapidly. Readers should verify the accuracy and relevance of the information in this book with up-to-date sources before making any financial decisions.

11. General Testimonial Disclosure

Testimonials featured in this book are from actual clients and non-clients who have voluntarily provided feedback regarding their experiences with our investment advisory services. These testimonials are not representative of all clients' experiences, and individual results may vary.

12. No Guarantee of Future Results

Past performance is not indicative of future results. While these testimonials reflect the experiences of our clients at a specific point in time, there are no guarantees that future results will be similar.

13. Client Consent

Clients and non-clients who have provided testimonials have given their consent for us to use their feedback for marketing purposes. Compensation or incentives has not been provided for these testimonials.

14. No Personalized Advice

The testimonials should not be interpreted as personalized investment advice. Each client's and non-client's financial situation and objectives are unique, and our services are tailored to individual needs.

15. Disclosure of Compensation

No client or non-client has been compensated for providing testimonials, and recommendations are not influenced by client feedback. My commitment is to act in your best interest.

16. Regulatory Compliance

This book strives to adhere to all relevant financial regulations and laws governing the use of client and non-client testimonials in our marketing materials. If you have any questions or concerns about our compliance practices, please contact us.

17. Full Disclosure

This book strives to provide accurate and transparent information about our services. If you have any questions or need more information about our client and non-client testimonials, please feel free to reach out to us.

18. Client Suitability

It's important to remember that testimonials may not be representative of your own investment experience or suitability. We recommend discussing your specific financial goals and circumstances with us before making any investment decisions.

19. No Obligation to Use Our Services

You are under no obligation to use our investment advisory services based on the testimonials or endorsements featured in our marketing materials. Your decision to engage our services should be based on your individual needs and preferences.

20. Changes or Updates

Testimonials may be updated or removed over time. The information presented in our marketing materials reflects the experiences of clients at the time of their testimonials.

21. Verification of Testimonials

Reasonable efforts have been made to verify the authenticity of the testimonials featured in this book. If you have any concerns about the accuracy or legitimacy of any testimonial, please let us know.

22. Paragon Portfolios Performance Disclosure

Investment performance reflects time-weighted, size-weighted geometric composite returns of actual client accounts and not back-tested hypothetical returns or performance. Returns reflect all material market and economic conditions for the time periods specified. Investment returns are net all management fees and transaction costs, and reflect the reinvestment of all dividends and distributions. The investment objective of the Top Flight, Fast Movers, Fundamental 20, and Liquidity Factor Models is capital appreciation and employs the use of various models to achieve this objective. The investment objective of the Managed Income Portfolio is income with a secondary objective of capital appreciation and employs the use of various models to achieve these objectives. Both Paragon Top Flight, Fast Movers, Fundamental 20, Liquidity Factor, and Managed Income Portfolios use various models that have changed from time to time and may change in the future, and the effect on performance results could be either favorable or unfavorable. U.S. Stock: Russell 3000 Total Return. Global Stock Ex U.S.: MSCI ACWI Ex USA Net Total Return. US Bond: Bloomberg US Aggregate. Global Bond: Bloomberg Global Aggregate. U.S. Real Estate: Dow Jones US Real Estate Index Total Return. The S&P 500 Index is a market-value weighted index comprised of 500 stocks selected for market size, liquidity, and industry group representation. The Barclays Aggregate Bond Index is a benchmark index made up of the Barclays Government/Corporate Bond Index. Benchmarks are used for comparative purposes only. The Paragon Top Flight, Fast Movers, Fundamental 20, and Liquidity Factor Models are not designed to track the S&P 500 Index or other referenced indices and will have results different from the benchmark. The Paragon Managed Income Portfolio is not designed to track the Barclays Aggregate Bond Index and will have different results. Past performance is not indicative of future results. Investments in securities involve the risk of loss.

ABOUT THE AUTHOR

At home with our children, Orem, Utah, 2017
Left to right: Austin, Shannon, Dave and Cathy, Kelli, Shawn, and Katie

Dave Young is an award-winning investment advisor, business owner, and entrepreneur. After starting a dozen successful businesses, Dave sold them and set out to invest the profits. When he couldn't find an investment company he trusted with his hard-earned money, Dave's entrepreneurial spirit kicked in, and he decided to do it himself. Today, Dave is the founder and president of Paragon Wealth Management, a top-ranked investment firm that currently manages approximately $150 million for 160 households and growing. Paragon's success has attracted local and national media attention.

Dave has a deep commitment to community service and philanthropy. In 2010, he cofounded the Live Your Dream Foundation to provide scholarships to single mothers. In 2021, Dave was elected mayor of Orem, Utah, a rapidly growing city of more than 100,000 people. Dave is also a trophy-winning big game hunter who has traveled from Alaska to Africa. Through his lifelong pursuit of adventure and excellence, Dave has learned that the valuable parallels between financial investing and big game hunting can help everyone, hunter or not, find true wealth—a genuinely happy, fulfilling, and financially abundant life.

Dave is a husband, father, and grandfather. His family is his greatest treasure.

Our grandchildren in our yard, 2017
*Back row, left to right: Allie Golladay holding baby Peyton Bunnell's hand,
Cathy, Charlotte Golladay in Dave's arms, Dave, Kali Edwards
Middle row: Rylie Bunnell, Charlee Young, Savannah Golladay, Jack Young
Front row: Kylie Young*

Now that you've read *Hunting for True Wealth*,
you can get more info and see photos
from my hunting adventures at
IdRatherBeHunting.com.

I look forward to connecting with you!

*A magnificent five-by-five mule deer with two eye guards and antlers bladed
in back. At thirty-one inches across, he had a classic box frame with the deepest
forks I'd ever seen and scored 208. Story in Chapter 10, hunting on
Nathan Ricks' 6,000-acre Buckhorn Ranch, Utah, fall 2010.*

www.ingramcontent.com/pod-product-compliance
Lightning Source LLC
Chambersburg PA
CBHW021628120626
46545CB00002B/446